Winning Politics

Winning Politics

A Handbook for Candidates and Campaign Workers

William L. Roper

Chilton Book Company

Radnor, Pennsylvania

To all politically ambitious young men and women—
and those not so young—who wish to make
government more responsive to the will of the governed

1 2 3 4 5 6 7 8 9 0   7 6 5 4 3 2 1 0 9 8

Contents

Preface

Whether you are considering a campaign for Congress and a lifetime career in politics or planning to help a friend who is running for your local school board or some other minor office, this book is for you. It is a practical how-to book, designed to aid the amateur as well as the professional in conducting a winning campaign.

The procedures and techniques for successful campaigning are basically the same, whether your campaign is for a local municipal office or for United States senator. They differ only in focus and procedural details. Commenting upon this similarity, Colonel Edward M. House, personal representative of President Woodrow Wilson, once said, "The secret of success in a presidential election is to forget it is a presidential election. There is a technique for electing a village constable. And there is a technique for electing a president. The formula in both cases is practically identical."

Yet while the techniques are in many ways identical, there are some important differences between local and statewide or nationwide campaigns. It is essential for the campaigner to understand how these campaigns may be unalike. This book describes both the similarities and the differences.

Success in politics, as in almost everything, follows certain definite rules, and the campaigner must know the rules before he or she can use them effectively or break them with impunity. These rules and techniques can be learned and applied—that is the thesis of this book.

The information presented in these pages is based upon practical, first-hand political experience in a wide variety of campaigns, ranging from school board and city and county offices to congressional, senatorial and gubernatorial. Actual cases are cited. In other words, this book does not deal in just abstract or academic political theory, but in the "nuts and bolts," the practical application of campaign-tested rules that win.

Among other things, this book will tell you:

how to analyze your chances, your qualifications, and your opponent's weaknesses;

how to get started;

how to formulate a campaign strategy or attack plan;

how to organize a political action group to promote and advance your candidacy;

how to create a winning image;

how to inspire the enthusiasm needed to assure election.

Remember, the rules of successful campaigning, the techniques and strategies recommended, are not guesswork or classroom theories. They have been tested and found effective in actual, successful campaigns.

They can help you win.

W. L. R.

Acknowledgments

I gratefully acknowledge the valuable information on many recent campaigns provided by *Campaign Insight*, a twice-a-month newsletter published by Campaign Associates, Inc., of Wichita, Kansas. It is the only publication of its kind in the United States. Acknowledged also is the aid of Hank Parkinson, president of Campaign Associates, *Campaign Insight* editor Linda Donlay, and former editor Susan Armstrong.

I likewise acknowledge my indebtedness to the many other expert tacticians I have worked with in California and Texas campaigns. They are too numerous to mention individually.

One book that I found particularly helpful in my early campaigning was *The Great Game of Politics* by Frank R. Kent, published by Doubleday, Doran & Company in 1931.

1
The Door Is Open

Consider the golden opportunities in politics—not just opportunities to enrich yourself, but to make your life count for more in human service. For many Americans, politics is seen as the modern-day Horatio Alger story of opportunity—a road to riches and power. It may be that for you, too, but it may also be the way to important public service and high adventure.

Instead of complaining about the sorry state of public affairs, do something about it. This is the challenge facing Americans, both young and old, today.

The door is open. Never before in our history have there been so many exciting and rewarding public offices to be filled by the elective process. And never before have there been fewer roadblocks in the way of ambitious persons, especially women and members of minority groups, who wish to seek public office. There are certain new financial restrictions, but racial and other social barriers are being torn down.

There was a time not long ago when party bosses or their ward lieutenants picked those who would become candidates for city council, state legislature, or even lower offices of local government. In some parts of America they still do. But on the whole, this dominant role of party chieftains is declining. Today ambitious, aggressive office seekers are asserting themselves, doing their own thing, occasionally in defiance of party leaders.

Don't let fear of politics as an unknown or "dirty" area hold you back. Politics has been called many things—a game, a science, an art, and also a stinking mess or rotten crooked business. Yet while some of its practitioners have given it a bad name at times, politics is actually just the organized citizen-action that is essential to any democratic government. Most thoughtful citizens see it this way and realize their responsibilities for making our system work.

THE NEWCOMER CAN WIN

With the dawn of a new day in participatory politics, an increasing number of women have been elected to posts of governor and senator, as well as to various state, county, and city offices throughout the United States. Even nineteen-year-old college students have been elected mayors and state assemblymen.

In 1976, in line with this new spirit in American politics, the United States elected the first president from the South since the Civil War. Jimmy Carter's election demonstrated once again that the door is open—that a citizen from a small town like Plains, Georgia, a man who at the start of his campaign was unknown to the great mass of American voters, could compete with nationally prominent political leaders and win.

There have also been other impressive demonstrations in recent years that political novices and virtual unknowns who had never previously sought political office could defeat well-known professionals.

How did they do it? What were their strategies and techniques? To answer such questions is one of the aims of this book.

In 1972, Maurene O'Connor, a twenty-five-year-old San Diego, California, high school teacher, was shocked to discover that many of her students were cynical about the democratic process in the United States. To convince them that they should have faith in government, she ran for a San Diego city council seat and won. How she did it is told in chapter 18.

Among the women winning high political office for the first time is Democrat Dixy Lee Ray, who was elected governor of Washington State in 1976. Although a newcomer to politics, she had served as former head of the Atomic Energy Commission. She defeated an experienced politician.

Another woman, also a political novice, made history in 1976. She was Rose Ann Vuich, an accountant and farmer who beat a well-known male legislator to become California's first woman state senator.

One of the most astounding triumphs in recent times by a political unknown was that of Dr. S. I. Hayakawa in California in 1976. Hayakawa was the first member of a minority race to win election to the United States Senate from California, and he did this in spite of tremendous obstacles.

Capitalizing on being an "outsider" and having no close association with the establishment or the Republican Party, the seventy-year-old Japanese-American, best known as a semanticist and retired college professor, first wrested the Republican nomination from three of California's leading Republican politicians. Robert H. Finch, former California lieutenant governor; Congressman Alphonzo Bell, an eight-term veteran; and John L. Harmer, former lieutenant governor, were the three big-name candidates vanquished in the primary by the political unknown. Finch reportedly spent in excess of $500,000 and Bell, $800,000, while Hayakawa's primary expenditures were only $166,000.

Hayakawa then proceeded to defeat the Democratic incumbent John Y. Tunney, who was a vigorous forty-two-year-old campaigner with strong financial support. Tunney was not only favored by a three-to-two Democratic registration, but had the endorsement of the state's largest daily, the *Los Angeles Times,* which is traditionally Republican. Despite this, Hayakawa polled 3,701,024 votes to Tunney's 3,464,583.

These West Coast elections, as well as several recent ones in eastern states, offer convincing proof that the door is open and that newcomers in politics can win.

YOUR OPPORTUNITY

In this book, you are told how to evaluate your assets and the odds against you. But don't let the odds scare you.

Discard your cynicism about politics. Think positively.

The door is open for clever, aggressive, self-confident campaigners who are sensitive to the voters' major concerns about jobs, inflation, housing, justice, better schools, and other basic issues that affect the daily lives of all of us.

Your opportunity for beginning a successful career in politics may lie near at hand. Many have found theirs by running for some low-level public office in their home community. Often the key to winning is in finding and making a campaign issue out of a problem that is worrying your neighbors.

Concerned citizens are usually only waiting for a leader. Strong, natural leaders seldom wait to be chosen. They take the lead. That is the way effective campaigns are born.

No, you don't have to be a lawyer, or even a high school graduate to run for public office. But an education will often help you to win, if you will learn the rules of the game. Public speaking ability, tact in human relations, ability to generate enthusiasm for a cause, and a flair for showmanship or publicity are the prime ingredients for political success.

As Plato said, "Let him who would move the world, first move himself."

2
Getting Started

You may get started in politics by organizing a reform committee or exposing corruption in local government. Or you can start by joining an established party and working as a volunteer in a party-sponsored campaign.

There are a number of other ways to start, and in this chapter you will see how Jimmy Carter, Harry Truman, Gerald Ford, Richard Nixon, and others did it. You will also see how some comparatively unknown persons—black and white, male and female—became successful candidates, with and without the support of party bosses.

THE PARTY AS SPRINGBOARD

Joining one of the major parties as a volunteer worker is the traditional method most often recommended. The experience can be very valuable. In addition to providing you an opportunity to learn first hand the practical mechanics of campaigning, it brings you into contact with politically minded persons. Such associations will become most helpful to you later when you become a candidate.

In return for your service to the party, the county or state committee may later pick you to run for office. There are several advantages in being selected as a candidate by your party. It usually assures some financial support and the assistance of volunteer workers.

Most party leaders—both Democratic and Republican—recommend starting as a party worker. It has worked well for many, but there is no certainty you will be selected to become the party's candidate for any office. In spite of your volunteer work, you may get passed by when an opening occurs.

What do you do in a case like that? You can take it lying down, or you can round up a group of your fellow party workers who are loyal to you and start your own campaign, independent of the party organization. Win your primary battle, and the party will most likely throw its weight behind you in the general election.

The Rise of Shirley Chisholm

Shirley S. Chisholm, the first black woman to win a seat in Congress, encountered a situation of this kind during her uphill fight for national recognition as a political leader. How she met the challenge and won points up an important lesson in practical politics.

Born in Brooklyn and educated in public schools in Brooklyn and later in Brooklyn College, where she was a member of the debating society, Shirley St. Hill Chisholm became a teacher after earning her M.A. in education at Columbia. Deeply concerned about civil rights, she became an active member of clubhouse politics in her Brooklyn assembly district and through hard work and aggressiveness worked her way up in New York politics.

Her first opportunity for public office came in 1964 when Thomas Jones, the local state assemblyman, accepted a judgeship. Chisholm decided she would run for the office vacated by Jones. When she mentioned the idea to the club's executive committee, she was told the subject would have to be given further study. "If you have to have a discussion," Chisholm told them, "have a discussion. But it makes no difference to me. I intend to fight."

Shirley Chisholm did fight. She won the 1964 primary and general election, winning the assembly seat. Because of reapportionment, she had to run again in 1965 and in 1966. In 1968 she ran for Congress from the 12th Congressional District of

New York, and won. In a hard-fought primary in the 1968 campaign, she had defeated James Farmer, a former national director of the Congress of Racial Equality. Her vote-getting ability led to her being chosen in 1972 as the Democratic vice-presidential candidate.

Debating skill and experience acquired in club politics in Brooklyn were prime ingredients in her success as a campaigner. These have made her an inspiring example of how to work and fight your way to the top, despite numerous handicaps.

How a Youth Beat the Odds

Today many young men and women are doing it just the way Shirley Chisholm did. They enlist as volunteers in a local political organization and use that association and experience as a spring-board.

Two recent examples come to mind. Jim (James L.) Chapman is one of them. Jim began working in Democratic campaigns in California when he was in the eighth grade, knocking on doors and passing out literature for candidates. On his eighteenth birthday he was appointed a member of the Democratic campaign committee, and a year later he was elected secretary-treasurer in his community of Susanville. A natural vote-getter, he was chosen high school junior class president and was later elected president of the Lassen Community College student body.

During all of this time, Jim was also speaking out on civic concerns—the need for a more effective police department, better streets, and other improvements he thought should be included in Susanville's city budget.

But when he announced his candidacy for a place on the Susanville city council, he found he had plenty of competition. Six other citizens, some experienced office holders, had filed for the two vacancies. To make his youthfulness work for him instead of against him, Jim adopted the campaign slogan, "A Voice for the Future," and began painting a picture of Susanville's future needs.

Attracted by Chapman's vision of civic improvements and a better city in which to live, many of his fellow students and numerous older citizens pitched in to help him. Since very little money was involved, the campaign was largely a volunteer effort —vote solicitation by telephone and door-to-door campaigning.

He won the council seat when he was only nineteen. He became mayor of Susanville when he was twenty-one. His work as a party volunteer and as an aggressive spokesman for civic improvements had paid off quickly in political advancement.

How a 19-Year-Old Beat a Veteran

Another young man who used the time-honored formula of working as a volunteer to learn electioneering is Mike Elconin of Wisconsin. In 1972, Mike, then only nineteen, made use of the political know-how he had acquired as a volunteer in judicial and congressional campaigns to defeat Joseph L. Jones, a five-term veteran, in a contest for Wisconsin's 16th district assembly seat. Since Jones, the incumbent, had won the office for five consecutive terms, he was considered virtually unbeatable.

But while doing house-to-house canvassing in the district, Mike discovered that many voters were dissatisfied with Jones. Much of the dissatisfaction stemmed from Assemblyman Jones' stout support of the trucking industry's use of large sixty-five-foot trucks, despite citizen protests. Wisconsin at the time had a high rate of highway fatalities, and the super-trucks were being blamed for many of them. In talking with voters in the 16th district, Mike found many citizens angry that Jones apparently ignored their complaints about highway safety.

A politically astute young man, Mike realized that this was a red-hot issue. And he decided to challenge Jones, a fellow Democrat, for the assembly seat. This meant a hard primary fight. It was like David taking on Goliath, Mike realized, because Jones was firmly entrenched with party leaders. A proven winner in his past campaigns, he was certain to get party endorsement. Moreover, Jones had strong support from COPE, organized labor's political action corps.

Mike, self-confident in spite of the tremendous odds favoring Jones, knew that a primary victory would be tantamount to victory in November over the Republican candidate, since the district was heavily Democratic in registration.

He began his campaign by calling together a number of his fellow workers and enlisting their cooperation. In a short time, he had an "Elconin for Assembly" committee organized. Signatures of sponsors were obtained, and he filed as a candidate. His friends assisted him in raising money, and with his team of volunteers, he began making house-to-house calls on the 2,500 homes of those he thought would vote in the Democratic primary. He had obtained the voters' home list while working in prior campaigns.

Continuing to emphasize highway safety and reminding the voters of Jones' legislative voting record in favor of the trucking interests, Mike used bumper stickers, window signs, and coffee hour talks to sell his campaign program. But the main thrust of his campaign was the house-to-house canvass, conducted by him and his volunteer workers.

Jones, lulled into complacency by the fact that his opponent was a nineteen-year-old "kid," did not think it was necessary to campaign hard. On election night, he was one of the most surprised politicians in Wisconsin, when the vote count showed "the kid," Mike Elconin, to be the winner.

OTHER WAYS TO GET STARTED

Mike Elconin won his first public office by finding an incumbent's political weakness and taking advantage of it. Another good way to start is by exposing corruption in local government or by speaking out on some issue of major concern.

Or you may follow what is often called the "Fuller Brush Routine," as did Jimmy Carter, shaking hands with a lot of voters, talking about governmental problems in which they are vitally interested, proposing solutions, and smiling a lot.

You may attract favorable attention and a devoted following as a radio or television commentator. Or if such a forum is outside your reach, you can speak before civic, public affairs, and church groups in your community. Jim Chapman, mentioned earlier, used that method effectively.

All of these routes have been followed with success. It's all a matter of achieving popular identity as a leader. Jerry Ford began doing it in Michigan as a football star, Richard Nixon as a champion debater at Whittier College. *Whether you start as a party volunteer or as an independent on your own, you must achieve popular identity as a leader.* You can do that by speaking out on public issues, shaking hands, and making friends.

Carter's Challenge

Usually it is best to run for a low-level, local office first. Jimmy Carter, for example, made his entry into politics by becoming a school board member and civic worker in his home community. From 1955 to 1962 he was chairman of the Sumter County (Georgia) board of education.

He first filed for elective state office in 1962 when he ran for a seat in the Georgia state senate. The ballot count indicated that his opponent had won by a few votes. Carter suspected trickery and filed suit challenging the count. Investigation disclosed that ballot boxes had been stuffed with votes in the names of dead persons and other non-voters. The court reversed the election, naming Carter the winner.

Carter's successful challenge of the vote count and the judicial ruling of vote fraud focused the spotlight on him, resulting in favorable publicity. From that beginning and his service in the Georgia state senate, he went on to become governor of that state.

Nixon's Successful Debate

It was Nixon's ability as a college debater that led him into politics back in 1946. A group of conservative Republicans—many of them in the banking and savings and loan business—were seeking an articulate young man to run in the 12th Congressional District of California against Congressman Jerry Voorhis, a liberal Democrat. Roy Day, Republican district chairman, had inserted a small announcement in newspapers stating that a candidate "with no previous experience" was wanted. While several prospects answered, none was chosen.

The group then tried to get Dr. Walter Dexter, former president of Whittier College, to run. He declined, but suggested a graduate of the college who had won local fame as a debater. Nixon, then on naval duty in Maryland, was telephoned and invited to become the group's candidate. He accepted the opportunity, returned to California, and his nomination petition was filed.

In the primary, Nixon soon encountered some unexpectedly tough competition from a young Fuller Brush salesman who had acquired skill in door-to-door canvassing. Attempting to handle his own publicity, Nixon also had problems with the press.

At this critical point in his political career he was fortunate in obtaining Bill Arnold, a Los Angeles publicist, as his press agent, and his fortunes began to change. Arnold was the son of Fred Arnold, political editor of the *Los Angeles Herald-Express* and one of the wisest political operators in southern California. As Nixon's standing improved due to professionally handled publicity, Murray M. Chotiner, regarded by many as southern California's cleverest political manager and publicist, became associated with his campaign. Chotiner soon became one of Nixon's most trusted advisers.

Nixon made effective use of his debating skills in a series of debates with Voorhis. A personable New Deal Democrat and the son of a millionaire, Voorhis had graduated Phi Beta Kappa from Yale, but he was no match for the Whittier College debater. Nixon sought to portray Voorhis as a radical because he had accepted campaign support from the CIO Political Action Committee. Voorhis was soon on the defensive. Victorious in this campaign in 1946, Nixon was to become nationally known as a crusader against communism.

Ford, the Home Front Republican

Gerald Ford, the Michigan football star, got his start in politics in a way somewhat similar to Nixon by being selected as a candidate for Congress by a small Republican club group. The outfit, known as the "Home Front Republicans," met frequently at the Cherrie Inn in Grand Rapids to discuss political candidates and issues. One of its principal objectives was the selection and promotion of young political talent.

The leader of the Home Front Republicans was W. B. "Doc" Ver Mculen, a Grand Rapids dentist, who had no political ambitions of his own but who for many years had fought to break the grip of Frank McKay and his machine on the Republican Party in Michigan. Since Ver Meulen and his associates believed Congressman Bartel J. Jonkman, who represented Michigan's 5th district, was a McKay man, they were seeking a candidate to run against Jonkman. They wanted a bright, young lawyer with a military service record. And they preferred a blond, who looked as though he might be of Dutch ancestry, since about half the voters in the district were Dutch.

Jerry Ford, who had become well known in Michigan as a football star, met those qualifications. Enlisting in the Navy in 1942, he had seen forty-seven months of active service, much on an aircraft carrier in the South Pacific during World War II. He had studied law at Yale.

So one day at a luncheon meeting in the Cherrie Inn, Ver Meulen informed Ford that he had been chosen to run against Jonkman in 1948. Ford, then 35, accepted the challenge and filed as a candidate.

Ver Meulen and the Home Front group saw to it that he got lots of publicity. They even had him photographed milking a cow in a 4-H Club contest. This picture proved to be effective in giving him a favorable image in the Dutch community where there were many dairy families. Ford defeated Jonkman, and went to Congress. This was the beginning of the political career that carried Ford to the presidency.

Truman's Machine Backing

Harry S. Truman also got his start in politics through a special kind of organization, referred to by the *Kansas City Star* as the "Tom Pendergast Machine." Thomas J. Pendergast, saloon owner, was widely known as a political boss of great influence in Kansas City politics. In 1921, Pendergast and his associates were seeking a smart young man with a good war record and a clean reputation to run for a Jackson County judgeship. The major responsibility of the office was supervising public works—road building and maintenance of county institutions. They wanted a friend in the office who could aid them in getting public contracts.

One of Boss Tom's nephews, Jim Pendergast, had served in Captain Truman's Battery D, 129th Field Artillery, 35th Division. He recommended his ex-captain to his uncle. Truman, then 37, was having financial problems. The little haberdashery he had opened in Kansas City with an army buddy was failing to show a profit. Informed that Pendergast would back him for the judgeship, Truman filed for the office.

With the influential organization supporting his candidacy, Truman beat his Republican opponent in 1922 and was elected. He was defeated in his bid for re-election, but ran again in 1926, winning a four-year term as presiding judge. County contracts for

$60,000,000 in public works were awarded, and Truman gained political strength.

Consequently, when he filed as a candidate for the U.S. Senate in 1934 on the Democratic ticket, he had strong Kansas City support, and won. In 1944 when he was being considered for the vice-presidential nomination, those opposing his nomination brought up the subject of his prior Pendergast association. Denying there was anything wrong in that relationship, Truman stoutly defended the Kansas City boss. He said, "Pendergast is a fine gentleman. Why, if you read the *Kansas City Star* you get the idea he had horns. Nothing of the kind. Tom Pendergast did a great deal of good. He was always helping people, even people who did nothing for him. He gave away huge amounts to charity. You could trust him. His word was his bond."

Despite Truman's defense, Pendergast and an associate, ex-Governor Guy B. Park of Missouri, were later sent to prison following conviction of involvement in a gigantic insurance fraud. Illegal voting practices in Kansas City during Pendergast's political reign were also revealed by a state investigation. Witnesses testified that names of dead persons, copied from tombstones, had been voted in Jackson County elections.

While Governor Park's association with Pendergast was disastrous, Truman was not seriously injured politically by his being a beneficiary of the machine's aid. Without Tom Pendergast's original boost, he might never have made it to the top. At that point in time, it was difficult to win public office in Missouri without Pendergast's backing.

The Young Lawyers

Young lawyers have often made triumphal entry into politics by prosecuting cases that made front-page news headlines.

Tom Dewey, while serving in an appointive position as U.S. attorney for the Southern District of New York, grabbed the national spotlight in 1935 when he began a two-year investigation and prosecution of organized crime in the state. In 1937 he was elected district attorney of New York County, and in 1942 became governor of New York State.

Dan Moody, a red-headed Texas attorney, followed a similar route to power by prosecuting the Ku Klux Klan as an illegal conspiracy. He became governor of the Lone Star State in 1926.

Earl Warren also won fame as a prosecutor of the Ku Klux Klan in California, but he made his initial entry into politics by cultivating the friendship and backing of Joseph Knowland, publisher of the *Oakland Tribune* and Republican boss of Alameda County. Elected district attorney through Knowland's strong support, his work as a vigorous prosecutor made newspaper headlines.

PUBLICITY: A MAJOR KEY

While Dewey, Moody, and Warren found their foothold and starting point in the legal profession, their initial political advancement was due mainly to one thing—sensational publicity of a favorable nature. At that time, lawyers could not legally advertise, but they could make news that was headlined.

And that is still one of the important elements for entry and advancement in politics. Publicity is a major key.

In recent years, an increasing number of radio and television commentators and newspaper reporters have been winning important political offices. Wilbert Lee O'Daniel, who once sold flour to Texas housewives by a noon-day broadcast over a Fort Worth radio station, was one of the first to win statewide political popularity by becoming a radio personality. When he entered the race for governor of Texas in 1938, he was opposed by many of the state's professional politicians. Thirteen, many of them prominent Democrats, filed to oppose him in the Democratic primary, which was decisive at the time because the state was solidly Democratic. They spoke of him contemptuously as the "Yankee-born, Kansas-reared" flour salesman.

But O'Daniel won, polling more than half the votes cast. He became governor without a run-off. Radio had demonstrated its merit as an effective springboard to high office.

FIND AN ISSUE AND GET MOVING

Yet you do not have to be a radio broadcaster, a lawyer, or a newspaper person to become a successful candidate. You do not even have to have a political boss or a party chieftain as a sponsor, although they are often helpful.

What you do need most of all is a sensitivity to the basic issues about which most of the voters in your area are concerned. You must also have a strong urge to take the lead in helping your friends and neighbors solve those problems. Without that incentive, you will be at a disadvantage in winning enthusiastic voter support.

Your first step if you decide to seek office is to select the office in which you can best serve and which seems most available. Then discuss the idea with friends who share your community's concerns and who can help you organize the nucleus of your campaign. *One of your first objectives must be to get a following. A large corps of volunteer workers is one of your best assurances of victory in any community campaign.*

Unless you are running as a party-favored candidate, you and your friends will have to circulate a petition to get your name on the nominating ballot. The number of names of registered voters needed and other requirements vary from state to state, so you may have to obtain legal advice to be certain this step is done right.

While a low-level local campaign can often be conducted effectively with a minimum of newspaper and radio advertising and very little, if any, television time, you will need money to finance your campaign. Your particular financial needs will depend upon the nature and scope of the campaign. Volunteer workers, if carefully trained, can be one of your most effective mediums for reaching the voters and getting your message to them.

Since most newspapers, published principally for profit, are seldom generous in giving a newcomer a lot of free publicity, you will need to find a hot issue of general concern and make news. There is nothing better than a good, fiery crusade against some public wrong to get headlines and arouse voters.

Find yourself an ogre to slay, an unjust tax burden or some form of official misconduct to assail. Or launch a campaign for a more efficient police department, better schools, or some other civic need. These are some of the ways you can make yourself stand out as a leader.

Successful campaigning is a science, using certain techniques and strategies to influence the voters. It is psychology in action combined with a lot of hard work, and it demands careful planning. The following chapters will help you develop your own blueprint for victory.

3
Weighing Your Chances

One of the first questions you must ask yourself when you consider becoming a candidate is "What are my chances?" There are certain well-established procedures for estimating your chances, but there is no way to do it with absolute certainty because several variables are involved.

For example, your chances depend largely upon four things: (1) voter approval of you vs. your opponent, (2) vote appeal of your program vs. that of your rival, (3) habitual voting habits of the area involved, and (4) effectiveness of your campaign vs. that of your opponent's.

You can obtain a quick estimate of your chances as based on no. 1 and no. 2 by conducting a sample opinion poll by telephone of a small percentage of the voters. But if you are a political unknown running against an incumbent who has "name recognition," the opinion poll on no. 1 would not be a fair test at the beginning of a campaign. Voters may know the incumbent's name, but know very little about him. You can check the voting habits of the area by examining past records on file at party headquarters, at a local newspaper, or at the public library. But there is no way to analyze no. 4 in advance of the actual campaign.

Don't be too quick to withdraw because you can't be certain of victory. A hard-hitting campaign on strong issues might completely change the picture.

QUESTIONS TO ASK YOURSELF

Here are the questions you should ask yourself in weighing your chances:

1. What are my qualifications? Do I have what it takes to win? What will be my weaknesses as a candidate? How can I neutralize their effect and impress voters that I am qualified?

2. Who will be my major opponent or opponents? What are their strengths and weaknesses as candidates?

3. What is the party registration of the area? Will my party affiliation be a handicap or an asset?

4. What is the voting pattern shown by recent elections? Will a similar trend prevail in the forthcoming election, or will some national or state campaign influence the pattern?

5. Can I get the money for an effective campaign?

6. Can I count on strong party support and volunteer help?

7. Can I expect any strong newspaper or other media support?

8. Is the time right, or is my campaign likely to be caught in an adverse landslide vote, favoring my opponent?

Of course, other factors are involved, but the above questions suggest the basic ones to be considered. The hardest question for you to answer will probably be "Am I qualified?"

Don't be too quick to down-grade yourself. Think positively about your qualifications. What if Napoleon had decided he could never be a general because he was only pint-sized and many of the soldiers in the French army were much taller? What if Demosthenes had decided he could never become a great orator and Greek leader because he had a shrill voice, weak lungs, and could not pronounce the letter *r*? By exercise and practicing speaking at the seashore with pebbles in his mouth, he developed his voice and became the most famous orator of all time. Most of us never achieve our full potential because we are afraid to try.

ATTRIBUTES OF A SUCCESSFUL CANDIDATE

Those most successful in politics are nearly always articulate, aggressive, and sensitive to the concerns of their fellow man.

They are also friendly and are good mixers. These are abilities that can be acquired to some degree.

Equally important is a sense of belonging to the area in which you are running and of being accepted by the voters as one of them. Ethnic prejudices are still strong in some areas and must be considered. But racial barriers are fading.

One point you must consider in your self-appraisal is your status as a registered voter. Are you registered in the district in which you plan to run? If not, you must register in time to qualify as a voter and candidate. The address you give in registering should be your home address, not a part-time or business one. Otherwise it may cause you trouble.

Occasionally a candidate will move into a new political subdivision to register there because surveys have convinced himself its voting pattern offers him a better chance of election. But usually a candidate fares better in a community where he is well known.

See if you can stand the test advocated by the late Murray Chotiner, one of California's best known political tacticians. Chotiner's rigid yardstick for measuring a candidate contained the following four points:

1. The candidate must be *clean*—on record, in his background, and in his personal life. The things the general public doesn't know about a candidate, the opposition either knows or will find out. They will bear down on these bad aspects of a candidate at some time in the course of the campaign.

2. The candidate must be *clear* on the issues. You can't fool the voting public very long—they catch on mighty quick. Too many candidates speak on both sides of an issue, and half the time you can't be sure just which stand they are taking.

3. The candidate must be *constructive*. He must stand for something. Usually, a successful candidate stands for one basic thing and travels throughout his community or constituency advocating his championship of this basic idea or project. All successful candidates seem to develop that indefinable "something" that appeals to the voters.

4. The candidate must be *courageous*. He must be willing to put on a fighting campaign. When you get a candidate who is a "milquetoast," the odds are that he is going to be defeated.

Chotiner's list of qualifications presents a tough challenge that some of the candidates he managed had difficulty meeting. Measure yourself and your opponent against his yardstick.

GETTING THE FACTS YOU NEED

There are numerous sources for the information you require in weighing your chances. If you are running for a high-level state or federal office, however, you will want the services of professional researchers and expert pollsters.

In a campaign for a local office or a community campaign, you can get most of the information you need from the following sources:

1. Local newspaper editors, political editors, and newspaper files containing clippings about politicians, past elections, etc.

2. Your local library. Many public libraries have clipping files and statistical reports compiled by the Governmental Affairs Institute. Some have issues of the *Handbook of Contemporary American Election Statistics,* compiled and edited by Richard N. Scammon, which contain data on county and precinct voting on national candidates.

3. Your political party headquarter's files on party registration and past voting trends.

4. City hall records, if you are running for a city office. The records will show voting records of office holders and voting trends in the city.

5. Members and files of the county bar association and its judicial candidates committee, in case you are running for a judicial office.

6. Members and records of parent-teachers' associations, school officials, teachers' organizations, and tax-payers' associations, if you are a candidate for the school board.

7. Friends in the banking business who may be able to learn about your opponent's campaign financing. In federal and in some state campaigns, financial contributions and expenditures must be reported. Also check on your opponent's credit rating.

8. The police department and sheriff's office. Check to see if your opponent has any arrest or criminal record on file.

9. The voting record of an incumbent office holder. Study your opponent's voting record carefully. If he is an incumbent judge, especially check two things: (a) has he ever been known to act as a judge in cases in which he might have been personally or financially interested? (b) has he been criticized for being too lenient and light-handed in sentencing criminal offenders, or too harsh? These are frequent criticisms of a judge's record that must be carefully investigated in weighing him as a political rival.

TAKE A CHANCE

After collecting your information, analyze it to the best of your ability. Unless your opponent appears clearly unbeatable, you should do as most politicians do—take a chance. As George Eliot so wisely wrote:

> No great deed is done
> By falterers who ask for certainty.

4
Investigating Your Opponent

One of the most important rules in successful campaigning for public office is to investigate your opponent thoroughly. That means getting the facts, the real low-down on him, not just rumors.

An investigation of this kind is absolutely essential because more voters vote *against* someone rather than *for* someone or something. This fact has been demonstrated in numerous campaigns. So you must find something, if possible, in your opponent's character, official record, or background that will cause a majority of the voters to cast their ballots against him. Since he is human, he is almost certain to have an Achilles' heel—a very special weak spot that makes him vulnerable.

His official record should be your special target, but you may find something objectionable in his conduct before he got into public life. It could be the unsavory reputation of his associates, a book he has written, or his war record. In some communities, it would be particularly damning if he were found to be a card-carrying communist at one time, or if he had been active in anti-American demonstrations. One southern California congressional candidate, who appeared almost certain of victory when nominated, was defeated upon it being revealed that he once was active in the Ku Klux Klan in New York.

CAMPAIGN ACCUSATIONS: HANDLE WITH CARE

Investigate your opponent, yes. But never try to capitalize on your opponent's personal life, that is, his marital problems or other areas in which the public welfare is not concerned. Efforts to do so will usually create voter sympathy for him and react against the candidate making the charge. In fact, you must always carefully weigh the effect of any critical statement you make against your opponent, even if you are absolutely certain of the facts. You must guard against saying anything that will create sympathy for him.

Democrat Gary Familian, a wealthy southern California businessman, made an error of this kind in his 1976 congressional race against Republican Robert K. Dornan. He publicized on radio a marital and child custody controversy between Dornan and Mrs. Dornan. This attempt to expose Dornan's personal life backfired and Familian lost the election. He had also attempted to link Dornan with the Ku Klux Klan, the John Birch Society, and violence that had developed in a clash over school textbooks in West Virginia in 1974. Denying these links and insisting that his involvement in the textbook controversy was as "a peace maker," Dornan filed suit against Familian for $15 million. The case has since been reported settled out of court.

Cases such as this one illustrate the danger of making campaign accusations unless absolutely certain of your facts and the public's probable reaction.

Failing to know your opponent's actual background can also cause one to make a costly mistake. During her 1942 campaign for Congress, Clare Booth Luce referred to her opponent, Congressman LeRoy Downs, as "the faceless man," who followed a Democratic "rubber-stamp" pattern. She did not realize that Downs had suffered a serious facial disfigurement in service during World War I and had undergone plastic surgery. This unfortunate mention of Downs' face cost her votes, although she won the election. Getting all the information you can about your adversary will protect you from making mistakes of this type.

Republican strategists made a serious error of this kind in the 1976 presidential campaign when a G.O.P. organization tried to exploit the confrontation between a black activist and Jimmy

Carter's Southern Baptist church in Plains, Georgia. When the deacons closed the doors of the church one Sunday and canceled services for the day because a Negro was seeking permission to join, a Republican campaign group mailed out thousands of letters to Negro and civil rights leaders calling attention to the incident.

But this attempted agitation of a racial issue backfired in favor of Carter. Many of the nation's black leaders remembered that it was Carter himself who had taken the lead some time ago in urging the church to open its doors to Negroes. When the presidential vote was later counted and analyzed, it was disclosed that more than 90 percent of the nation's black vote had been cast for Carter.

SCRUTINIZE YOUR RIVAL'S RECORD

If your opponent has ever held or is now holding public office, one of the first things to check is his official record. How has he voted and spoken out on issues about which the voters are now concerned? Have any of his public actions been publicly criticized or investigated by civic or governmental agencies? Has he ever been indicted or accused of involvement in a racket of any kind? Who are his closest associates, advisers, and financial sponsors? And who are his known political enemies? (These enemies may be helpful in supplying you with tips, but be careful about being seen with them. They may have axes to grind and being seen with them might cause others to regard you with suspicion.)

Most professional campaign managers believe in exploring every facet of the opposition candidate's background. And there may be certain episodes in his personal life that are not exempt from scrutiny and possible exploitation. Drunk driving and acts of an immoral nature that appear to affect public morality are in this category. Yet one must keep in mind that any attack that violates voters' sense of fairness can be more harmful than productive.

The danger is not so much in making the investigation, but in the use you make of the facts you discover. Any charge you make must be sufficiently substantiated to convince the voters. Otherwise, your opponent may successfully defend himself as being the victim of a smear, and you are labeled a mud-slinger.

COMPILING A DOSSIER

Early in your campaign, begin to compile a dossier on your adversary, recording in it all available information about him, and underlining the more pertinent with red ink. It should include all news clippings of his speeches and actions, official and otherwise, that you can find. If he has been mentioned editorially, clip and file the editorials.

Much information of this kind can be obtained from newspaper morgues (reference libraries of newspapers), that is, if you can gain access to them (they are usually guarded jealously by the owners). Often a member of the news staff can be induced to make copies of the desired information for you.

Use a Clipping Service

If you are campaigning for a state office, you should subscribe to a regular clipping service. The Press Intelligence Service, Inc., 734 Fifteenth Street NW, Washington, D.C. 20005, performs that service for several politicians in that area. It will clip newspapers in other states for a regular fee plus a small unit charge for each clipping. Most larger cities and many of the state capitals have services of this kind.

But do not rely totally upon any commercial clipping service to keep you informed. Assign a staff worker to read all of the papers in your area. Everything about your opponent and his associates should be clipped and filed. You might also alert your friends in nearby areas to clip and mail you anything pertaining to the campaign. Record his radio and television speeches during the contest.

Additional Sources of Information

There are many places you can go to besides newspapers for information about your opponent. Some public libraries keep files on persons of prominence. They will usually permit you to make photoprints.

In large cities, business, manufacturers', and labor organizations, consumers' associations, and various reform groups maintain files on state and federal legislative members. The offices of these trade and labor organizations are excellent sources of information, since many of them are engaged in lobbying activities and employ professional investigators and research staffs to keep constant watch on what the lawmakers are saying and doing. If you can convince a top official of one of these organizations that you are on his side, he may supply you with some effective campaign ammunition, provided that your opponent is not one of their favorite people.

If your opponent is a member of Congress, you can check his vote on all bills that are of special interest to the voters in your constituency, and you can also read his remarks in the *Congressional Record*. The Commerce Clearing House publishes a *Congressional Index* weekly, and copies are on file in most public libraries. This index lists information on all public bills and resolutions before Congress. It gives a brief statement of the purpose of the bill, date of introduction, and committee references. The *Congressional Quarterly,* also published weekly and on file in most public libraries, supplies comprehensive information on current congressional activity.

Using information available from these sources, Murray Chotiner, when campaign manager for Richard M. Nixon, cited the vote of Congresswoman Helen Gahagan Douglas to defeat her in 1950 when she and Nixon were locked in a bitter campaign for a U.S. Senate seat. Headlining the charge, "Douglas-Marcantonio Voting Record," Chotiner alleged that Mrs. Douglas had voted 354 times in line with Marcantonio, an ultra-leftwing Congressman from New York.

Another source of information that you must not overlook in checking your adversary is the League of Women Voters, which has become increasingly alert and influential. A national organization, it has active units throughout the United States. Still another source is the Ralph Nader Congress Project: Citizens Look at Congress. It provides biographical data on members of Congress and their stands on consumer issues. Your local consumer groups, the chamber of commerce, and better business association may also be helpful.

You should also check with your rival's former employers to see if they consider him unreliable. Also, if the personnel officer is willing, get a peek at your opponent's personnel file. You must not neglect to check the court records, either. Check to see if your opponent has ever been arrested, sued, or is at the present moment involved in litigation. Has he ever failed to pay a state income tax?

In chapter 3, "Weighing Your Chances," one procedure was suggested for checking a judge's record or standing as a candidate. This was to talk with the secretary of your local bar association. In addition, go through the court records in the county clerk's and probate clerk's offices. You may find that the judge has been required at some time to list his property. Does he own stock in some company which has had litigation before him, and did he fail to disqualify himself?

Investigation disclosed that one Los Angeles County judge had been ordering litigants to deposit funds, impounded for various reasons, in a bank in Santa Monica in which he owned a controlling interest. Another Los Angeles County judge got into trouble by sentencing a man to prison, then marrying the man's wife while her ex-mate served his term. One of the most recent to fall into disfavor in the Los Angeles area was a judge arrested for drunken driving. Although he filed for re-election, he withdrew shortly before election day in 1976.

The most common complaint against judges, however, is that they are either too lenient or too harsh in their sentences. Letters to the editor frequently voice such complaints.

HAS HE WRITTEN A BOOK?

If your opponent has ever written a book, you are probably in luck. For it is generally conceded that a politician who has written a book may have sewn the seeds of his own destruction. Remember the wail of an ancient politician, "O, that mine enemy wouldst write a book."

Upton Sinclair, author of several books of social reform, collided head on with this fact of political life in 1934 when he ran unsuccessfully for governor of California on his EPIC (End Poverty in California) plan. His enemies dredged up quotations from his best-known books and hurled them at him, quoting passages to inflame group prejudices against him.

Ironically, several of Sinclair's books had rendered notable public service. His book *The Jungle* had played a prominent role in inducing President Theodore Roosevelt to initiate reforms cleaning up unsanitary conditions in the nation's stockyards and slaughtering plants.

James G. Blaine's authorship of *The Mulligan Letters* helped defeat him when he ran for the presidency in 1884.

Of course, if you are running for mayor, city council, or sheriff, you are not likely to find that your opponent has written a book that will damn his chances. But he may have written a letter to the local paper or said something in public that will. For instance, if he has made one kind of a statement or promise before a labor organization and said something of an opposite or contradictory nature before a group of employers, you may have something. Contradictory statements damage his credibility.

THE USE OF SPIES

In important state and federal campaigns, spies are often planted in the enemy camp. For instance, in Nixon's last big "Hurrah," campaign manager Murray Chotiner arranged for a clever young woman, posing as a news correspondent, to infiltrate the press corps accompanying the Democratic presidential candidate, George McGovern, on his campaign tour. She kept the Nixon team advised daily on what was occurring.

This tricky procedure is not particularly novel or unusual. Spying of some form is customary in most campaigns. The Watergate scandal illustrates the danger.

The safe rule in politics is this: *investigate your opponent thoroughly,* but do it carefully.

5
Finding the Basic Issues

At the very beginning of your campaign you must try to find the main issues, the problems of major concern to the voters you hope to win. And you must decide which of these basic issues will have the greatest vote-getting appeal in your campaign area. That is the issue you must hammer on and exploit in every way possible.

Your main issue may be the corrupt or inefficient record of your opponent if he is an incumbent. It is almost certain to be a problem or situation in some way related to the present conduct of the office you seek.

For instance, if you are a candidate for city council, the issue may concern some defect in city service that needs correction. Your city may need: better street lighting for safety; improved police protection and more night patrols; street paving to eliminate potholes; safer school crossings; noise abatement regulations; a recreational program to reduce juvenile delinquency; improved fire protection equipment and training; a more up-to-date public transportation system; better school bus service; a new park, library, or community building; reduction in city taxes; safeguards for the city water supply; a new sewer system; an improved garbage collection system; modern health service; or paramedic emergency service.

Once you find the major public concern, you can organize and start a campaign by proposing a reasonable solution, as Jim Chapman did to win election to the city council of Susanville, California. In other words, you become a convincing spokesman for a cause. Many important reforms have started just that way.

ISSUES CHANGE WITH CONDITIONS

It is an ageless axiom of practical politics that most voters think first in terms of their own self-interest. Jobs, inflation (meaning higher prices for food, clothing, and housing), taxes, and energy (for heating, transportation, and industry) are currently matters of major concern. As long as unemployment remains at a high level nationally, jobs and everything related to employment will continue to concern a large number of voters. Most political analysts agree that unemployment played an important role in the 1976 elections.

As conditions change, so do the concerns of the voters. Consequently, you must keep alert to changes in social and economic life or you will find you are campaigning on outdated issues and in opposition to public opinion. Long-time office holders, trying to maintain consistency with their past policies or record, occasionally make this suicidal mistake. They grow insensitive to the changing problems and the thinking of their constituents. In running against one of these archaic moss-backs, you can point to this insensitivity as an issue and call for a change.

One thing that seldom changes, however, is the voter's resentment of high taxes. It is almost perennial. Yet Americans will often vote for higher taxes to assure national defense, or for better fire or police protection.

If, as a candidate, you propose any program that may result in higher taxes, you will have to justify and explain it fully. Your opponent may make an issue of cost and center his fire on it, so you'll have to consider this possibility before championing any program difficult to defend.

Public Safety vs. Industry

In recent elections, consumerism and environmental issues have become subjects of greater voter concern, but they have been defeated or eclipsed in most contests by the "job issue." Loss of jobs has been raised as an effective argument to block governmental closing of plants that are polluting lakes, rivers, and the air we breathe. It would appear that residents of a community largely dependent upon industrial employment are often more concerned about maintaining job security than they are about obtaining governmental protection from a source of hazardous pollution. This situation may change in the future.

One might think that the danger of cancer-causing radioactivity from nuclear power plant accidents and the plants' unsolved waste disposal problem would be a viable safety issue. But when six states voted on the safety issue in 1976 to decide whether the construction of additional atomic plants would be permitted without greater safeguards, the safety advocates lost. A combination of power plant companies, nuclear reactor manufacturers, and big oil companies spent millions of dollars in advertising—a virtual public relations blitz which defeated the proposed regulations.

Another major issue involving industry versus the health of the American people has caused considerable controversy in recent years. It is the use of the cancer-causing chemical hormone, DES (diethylstilbestrol), a growth stimulant used in fattening beef cattle. Government tests have shown that use of DES caused cancer in animals. In August, 1972, the Food and Drug Administration announced that the oral use of DES would be prohibited after January 1, 1973. Representatives of the cattle industry and manufacturers of the hormone took legal action to block the FDA ban. And a federal court nullified the ban on the technical ground that no prior hearing had been held.

Use of DES as a cattle-feed additive continued and was the source of controversy not only in Congress, but between the United States and Canada, which had banned importation of DES-produced beef. Congress voted in 1975 to prohibit the use of DES as a growth stimulant for beef cattle until it can be determined scientifically that eating beef from animals fed or implanted with the drug will not cause cancer. Congressional action may not have settled the issue with finality. And if you are running for office in an area where most of the cattle are fattened for market in feed lots, instead of on the open range, you might find it politically dangerous to advocate a permanent ban on the use of DES in cattle feed.

Nevertheless, the public's health is always a valid concern. That this is widely recognized both by voters and legislators is shown by various laws enacted in recent years banning smoking in public places.

School Board Issues

In most school board campaigns, the major issues are taxes (property owners complain they are too high); busing to achieve integration; teachers' salaries; use of controversial textbooks; teaching methods; building costs; disciplinary practices; and complaints that classes are too large.

Court-ordered school busing to achieve racial integration is, in many communities, a hotly contested issue, even though there is little that a school board official can do. While a candidate can say he favors or disapproves of busing, all he may be able to do is to accept a judge's opinion or appeal it.

On the issue of school costs, the teachers and the parent-teachers' organizations will usually favor the increased school budget, while taxpayers and property owners' associations may oppose it. To get a clear view of the budget issue, you will have to talk to both the teachers' groups and the taxpayers.

In several parts of the country, parents of school-age children are urging a return to old-fashioned fundamentals like the three R's. This might be an issue in your community.

DON'T SCATTER YOUR SHOTS

In most city and county campaigns, you strengthen your chances of winning by concentrating on one or two basic issues. If you have enough zeal or enthusiastic campaigning ability, you may be able to sell an issue that is not widely popular. But it is always easier to win if you are championing a cause which has wide support.

Still, in almost every campaign, one sees candidates wasting their energies trying unsuccessfully to promote a minor issue or unimportant idea while neglecting major issues. Or they permit the main issue—the thing in which a majority of the voters are interested—to become buried in a mass of trivia. Trying to campaign on too many issues is dangerous. In doing this you scatter your shots. Concentration on the big, primary issue is always more effective.

KEEP ABREAST OF THE NEWS

Every politically ambitious person should keep currently informed regarding campaigns and issues by reading such news magazines as *Newsweek, Time,* and *U.S. News & World Report.* It will also be helpful to read the opinion magazines, *New Republic, Nation, American Opinion Magazine, Conservative Digest, National Review, The Progressive, Washington Monthly,* and *Human Events.*

There is only one national publication that is devoted entirely to campaigning—both techniques and strategies, and how candidates are using them. It is *Campaign Insight,* published by Campaign Associates, 408 Petroleum Building, Wichita, Kansas 67202.

If you are planning to run for Congress, there is one daily publication you should read regularly. It is the *Congressional Record.* While some ridicule it as a waste of paper, it does contain much vital governmental information and provides a picture of what Congress is supposed to be doing.

Reading your daily paper is, of course, a must. Regardless of what office you are thinking of running for, it is essential that you know what is happening in your community and the world. Take time to read the editorials and the letters to the editor. In them, you will often find those winning issues.

CONSULT YOUR CONSTITUENTS

Finding an issue is fairly simple in a city, county, or school district. It is largely a matter of conducting a careful survey, talking with as many concerned citizens as possible, and reading the editorials and letters to the editor in your local newspaper. You can then check the comparative rating of interest in various local issues by conducting a telephone or postcard survey. If you have a natural sensitivity to what concerns your neighbors, it will be a great help.

In state and federal campaigns, more elaborate techniques are required in sampling public opinion. Professional pollsters are nearly always employed for gathering information on issues in these campaigns for higher office.

One of the best ways to find out what the voters in your area believe to be the issues is to send out a questionnaire. Many members of Congress and state legislatures now use this method. Here is a sample of a questionnaire mailed out to his constituents by a member of Congress:

QUESTIONNAIRE

Name _____

Address _____

Phone Number _____

1. Would you favor delaying pollution controls on cars and industry in order to conserve fuel?   YES ___ NO ___
2. Would you favor gun registration as a way of controlling guns without prohibiting law-abiding citizens from owning firearms?   YES ___ NO ___
3. Should Congress and the President exercise tighter control over the CIA and FBI?   YES ___ NO ___
4. Do you believe federal health programs, such as Medicare and Medicaide, have been effective?   YES ___ NO ___
5. Do you feel that government involvement in private industry, such as price controls, safety and health requirements, environmental standards, minimum wages, and consumer protection, should be (mark one only please)
   a. eliminated?   YES ___ NO ___
   b. maintained?   YES ___ NO ___
   c. increased?   YES ___ NO ___
   d. reduced but not eliminated?   YES ___ NO ___
   e. no opinion   YES ___ NO ___
6. The next five years could well determine if the U.S. can turn the corner on energy independence. To achieve this goal, do you most favor (please mark only one answer)
   a. nuclear development?   YES ___ NO ___
   b. off-shore oil drilling?   YES ___ NO ___

   c. energy efficient cars and appliances?   YES __   NO __
   d. crash development of alternate sources
      of energy such as solar, tidal, geo-
      thermal?   YES __   NO __
7. Which issue affects you and your family
   the most? (please mark only one answer)
   a. the cost of living   YES __   NO __
   b. crime   YES __   NO __
   c. unemployment   YES __   NO __
   d. energy   YES __   NO __
   e. pollution   YES __   NO __
   f. tax reform   YES __   NO __
   g. other—additional comments _____

To learn how the voters in his district felt about a number of issues, a California state senator sent a questionnaire to his constituents asking them to rate the issues in order of priority. He included one form for both husbands and wives, but it was so written that both could express their ideas.

QUESTIONNAIRE

	HIS	HERS
Inflation, the economy	—	—
Unemployment	—	—
Consumer legislation	—	—
Malpractice insurance for doctors	—	—
Energy shortages	—	—
Environment	—	—
School financing	—	—
Transportation	—	—
Senior citizens programs	—	—
Collective bargaining for public employees	—	—
Welfare reform	—	—
Low cost housing	—	—
Quality and cost of medical care	—	—
Crime	—	—
Tax reform	—	—
City development	—	—
Land use	—	—

Many of the voters, both men and women, rated jobs or un-employment, inflation or the high cost of food, and crime—especially crimes of violence—as the major issues. Their opinions varied as to which of these three led in importance. Women showed more concern about the higher food prices, since they do most of the grocery shopping. Men indicated a slightly higher concern over unemployment. Although the legislator submitting this questionnaire put crime far down on the form, many of the voters living in urban areas rated it as the no. 1 problem.

Since not all voters respond quickly to a questionnaire such as this, you may find it advisable to draw up a simple questionnaire of your own and either employ local students or get volunteers to take it door-to-door asking questions.

Many citizens like to be consulted about issues and are happy to give you their opinions. Some will feel flattered that they are being asked. And they will be inclined to look with favor upon your candidacy because you or one of your representatives sought their ideas on these subjects of mutual concern.

But after collecting a good sampling of opinion in your area, you will have to analyze the answers carefully. Much as you might wish to do so, you cannot make the issues. You can only discover them and build your campaign around them. As James A. Garfield, the twentieth president of the United States, said, "Real political issues cannot be manufactured by the leaders of parties, and cannot be evaded by them. They declare themselves, and come out of the depths of that deep which we call public opinion."

With the development of the science of polling public opinion, politicians are becoming more adept at discovering the basic concerns of voters, out of which issues grow. You will find clues to those concerns in the news headlines and in the letters disgruntled citizens write to the editorial page.

To summarize, you find the basic issues by:

1. Being sensitive and alert to the thinking of the voters of your area.

2. Talking with a segment of the population to learn their major concerns.

3. Reading the newspapers and listening to radio and television commentators.

4. Checking the opinion polls against your own research among voters.

5. Reading the letters to the editor in the newspapers to see what citizens find disturbing.

6. Mailing out questionnaires asking the voters what they believe are the main issues.

7. Having volunteer or employed helpers go door-to-door making opinion surveys to find major concerns.

6
Organizing Your Staff and Raising Money

Your next step, now that you've found the main issue and discovered some of your opponent's political weak points, is to select the key members of your campaign staff and start raising money for a hard-hitting campaign.

YOUR CAMPAIGN ORGANIZATION

Virtually every campaign needs a publicity director, campaign manager, and treasurer. These executives are basic. In a major state or federal campaign, you will, of course, need the services of many additional executives and specialists.

The Publicity Director

No one should consider running for president or for city dogcatcher without a publicist.

You will need one to write the first announcement of your candidacy and get it into the media. That person will also write and release all of the publicity you must have in order to win. If you can find an experienced news writer, male or female, who not only has good relations with the working press but who has some understanding of political campaigning, you will be fortunate. The requirement is more than ordinary news writing ability. It calls for tact and the ability to create the right image for the candidate and sell his key issue to the voters.

The responsibilities of your publicist are described in greater detail in chapter 12.

The Campaign Manager

For campaign manager, you will need someone who is completely loyal to you and your cause and who has both political and executive experience. Actually the duties of a campaign manager are somewhat like those of a general, although he or she directs a campaign of psychological warfare instead of a military one.

One point has to be settled early in the campaign. Who will be in charge of what? In most campaigns, the campaign manager is in charge of the day-to-day operation but clears all important questions of strategy with the candidate. This problem of authority and responsibility needs clarification at the start of the campaign to avoid misunderstandings. Some political strategists argue that the manager should be given complete authority to direct every facet of the campaign and its strategy, but it is this writer's opinion that a divided command, shared by the candidate and the manager, is usually more successful.

During the past thirty years, a number of women have demonstrated almost uncanny ability as especially gifted campaign managers. Sam Yorty, former mayor of Los Angeles and before that a U.S. Congressman and member of the California legislature, owed much of his political success to the late Edith Chambers, who was widely recognized for her political genius. In politics one should never underestimate the capabilities of women, who are generally credited with keener intuition than men. Intuitiveness and sensitivity to issues can be decisive factors in winning elections.

The Treasurer

Your treasurer will be a key member of your staff. He or she must be experienced, competent, and honest. For more on the treasurer's responsibilities, see "State and Local Regulations" and "Questionable Sources of Money," below.

The Campaign Chairman

The campaign chairman is usually chosen for his or her name; in other words for his or her influence, reputation, and respectability. The person selected should be well known among your constituents, a leader in your community.

The chairman is not just a figurehead. He or she takes an active part in helping plan your campaign, participates in all board meetings, and volunteers his or her expertise when needed. Lawyers are frequent choices for campaign chairmen—a prominent and eminently respectable business leader would be another possibility—but in many local campaigns, the position is filled by the candidate himself.

The Secretary

Choice of a secretary is important. The secretary will usually serve as receptionist at campaign headquarters, handle the correspondence, answer the questions of voters who call to ask where their polling places are located, and explain your stand on issues.

Another responsibility of the secretary is to try to recruit volunteer workers from among persons phoning or visiting headquarters. A volunteer often assists the secretary in clipping and filing newspaper articles pertaining to the campaign.

Although volunteer workers should be able to handle much of the clerical work in a minor campaign, in most campaigns, you will need to employ some experienced stenographic assistance.

Campaign Headquarters

For campaign headquarters, you can choose a centrally located space in a downtown hotel or office building, or you can, perhaps, obtain a vacant store space free. The store site can be advertised to passing traffic with a large banner or sign, proclaiming it as your campaign headquarters.

If you are trying to run a local campaign on a very tight, economy budget, you may persuade a local business supporter to loan you desks, chairs, typewriters, and filing cabinets to equip your campaign headquarters. Yet even if you can get these essentials contributed, you'll need stationery, stamps, and some telephone service. You can reduce your phone bill by getting a pay phone installed, as did Ray Gonzales, a political science teacher who won election to the California legislature with an economy campaign. He and his workers did their phone vote-soliciting from their home phones.

HOW MUCH MONEY WILL YOU NEED?

Jesse Unruh, a former Democratic boss in California politics, has been quoted as saying, "Money is the mother's milk of politics." All politicians concede it is important. It is one of the essentials in most campaigns.

Yet it is not always the man with the most campaign money who wins. For instance, Ray Gonzales, a political science professor at California State in Bakersfield, California, spent only $21,000 in defeating incumbent Kent Stacey for a seat in the state assembly. Stacey, a Republican, reportedly spent $100,000. The state's Democratic Caucus did not give Gonzales any money until after he had won.

Gonzales' secret weapon was a lot of volunteer help that made up for the lack of money. At the start of his campaign, he and his volunteers held a $3-a-plate barbecue. Eight hundred persons attended. Just before the general election, they held another, charging $5 a plate. It attracted 1,200 patrons.

The bigger the office you are running for, of course, the more money you will need. To win election to a state or federal office, you will have to use television and hire professional help—and that is usually very expensive.

But if the office you seek is a city or county one, you may be able to rely largely on volunteer help and conduct a successful campaign on a minimum budget. Regardless of what office you have as your goal, however, you are going to need money for campaign literature, newspaper and radio advertising, clerical and possibly professional assistance, and other customary campaign expenses. And campaigning costs have been growing year by year.

Costs of campaigns vary greatly throughout the country, and one of the first things you must decide is how much you expect your campaign to cost. It will depend upon the number of voters you will have to reach in your campaign area, the importance of the office sought, and how much is usually spent in getting elected to that particular office. Your local party officials should be able to supply you with fairly accurate information on those points. And in case the office is a state or federal one, official records purporting to report campaign expenditures will be on file.

A campaign for a minor local office can cost $1,000 or less. But in case some power or a special interest is involved, or a highly emotional issue is at stake, the cost may run considerably higher. In rural areas, a campaign for the House of Representatives usually does not exceed $35,000 and might even be as low as $20,000, while in a heavily populated or metropolitan area, the costs might easily exceed $50,000. California candidates for Congress often spend in excess of $70,000. In 1976, Louis Brutocao, a prosperous Covina, California, businessman, spent $171,598 in trying unsuccessfully to defeat Congressman Jim Lloyd, who reported spending only $87,451.

Campaigns for the U.S. Senate cost much more in California than do the lower house contests. Congressman Alphonzo Bell spent in excess of $800,000 in an unsuccessful primary bid for a California seat in the U.S. Senate in 1976. That race was won by Dr. S. I. Hayakawa.

You may have to put some of your own money in the campaign fund to get things started. Brutocao initially contributed a substantial amount to his campaign. Both Lloyd and Brutocao received financial aid from their party coffers. The Democratic Congressional Committee gave Lloyd $4,000, and the Democratic State Central Campaign Organization contributed $3,000. Brutocao was given an even larger amount by Republican party organizations that had marked Lloyd for political liquidation.

But party organizations are often reluctant to invest heavily in a political newcomer who has not proved her or his vote-getting capability.

CAMPAIGN CONTRIBUTIONS AND THE LAW

There are several successful ways of raising money, *but before you start collecting you should obtain good legal advice on the current legal restrictions on campaign financing and also select someone you can trust to serve as campaign treasurer.*

Federal Limitations

Under the rather sweeping and complicated rules of the Federal Election Commission Act of 1974 and its amendments, strict limits on contributions, spending, and certain modified requirements for full reporting of campaign financing were imposed on candidates *for federal office.*

The 1974 law set a maximum contribution per individual donor of $1,000 for each primary, runoff, special, or general election. No donor could legally give more than a total of $25,000 to all federal candidates and political committees in any one election year.

A political committee (such as a lobbying or public interest group) could, under the law, give up to $5,000 in each election. Yet independent state divisions of these political lobbying or public interest groups could also make $5,000 donations. Actually there is no limit on the total amount such committees can donate in one election year, nor on the amount they can give to party organizations backing federal candidates. Consequently, the regulations that prevailed in 1976 have come under sharp attack because they have not solved the problem of freeing federal elections from the monetary influence of lobbyists and seekers of special privilege.

State and Local Regulations

If you are running for a city, county, or state office, the federal regulations, mentioned above, do not apply. But many states have also adopted fairly stringent regulations governing campaign financing for state offices, and you will have to work under the regulations governing your area. If you are unfamiliar with them, check them out with an attorney.

One of the most common offenses committed in campaigns, whether operating under federal or state regulations, is failing to file a campaign financial report in time. Often this delinquency is due to ignorance of the filing dates, but it is also frequently a result of the treasurer's failure to keep clear, correct records. These reports must be accurate and carefully prepared. They cannot be dashed off in a last-minute rush to meet a deadline.

Questionable Sources of Money

Even if you are not seeking a federal office and are free of strict restrictions, you will have to exercise care in where you get your campaign money. Otherwise it may become a scandalous issue.

An example comes to mind. During the late John Dockweiler's campaign for district attorney of Los Angeles County, which is a nonpartisan office, his campaign treasurer accepted a $10,000 contribution from "Bugsy" Siegel, a notorious gangster. It later became a subject of sensational embarrassment to Dockweiler, since Siegel was under criminal investigation at the time.

Cases such as this point up the importance of being very careful in your choice of a treasurer or financial chairman. She or he must be a person whom you can trust implicitly. In a major state or federal campaign, you will need both a finance chairman and a treasurer. You will need only a treasurer in a minor campaign, but the person chosen for this very responsible position must not only be experienced in financial matters, but one who has good sound judgment and a reputation for honesty.

In addition to assisting in collecting funds, the treasurer will be responsible for the day-to-day financial operations of the campaign—receiving, controlling, expending, and reporting funds. This entails filing any required legal reports within the specific time limits on proper tax forms.

FUND COLLECTION TECHNIQUES

First off, one point in money-raising needs special emphasis: *start your money raising early. Beat your rivals. Get to the big contributors before they do.* Some candidates for federal office begin raising money two years prior to starting their campaigns. In a local campaign, you should start raising money at least three months prior to announcing your candidacy.

The problem of getting money for a minor campaign is much simpler than collecting a huge war chest for a big federal or state campaign, but some of the techniques used are the same. Fund collections are usually made by personal solicitation, direct mail, telephone solicitation, newspaper advertising, radio and sometimes TV commercials, barbecues, cocktail and coffee parties, and rallies or special events.

Dick Viguerie, owner of the Richard A. Viguerie Co. in Falls Chuch, Virginia, raised more than $4.8 million for George Wallace mainly by direct mail prior to Wallace's 1976 primary campaign for the presidency. Viguerie, who had formerly raised money for Republican candidates, used what has been described as the largest mailing list of conservative voters in the United States.

In 1974 when Ramsey Clark ran for the U.S. Senate in New York, he reportedly collected a quarter of a million dollars from 12,000 supporters by running ads in the *New York Times*. Hamilton Fish, director of fund raising for Clark, said $8,000 spent in advertising in the *Times* would give the campaign a profit of about $14,000.

You can also collect money for your campaign by advertising in your local newspaper, if you can come up with several good, persuasive, convincing reasons why readers should contribute.

Collecting funds is a "selling job," whether you do it by newspaper, radio, direct mail, or personal appeal. You have to convince prospective contributors that by helping finance your campaign, they are serving the best interests of their party, the community, and themselves.

In collecting funds for a small community-type campaign, you will usually begin by getting contributions from friends, relatives, and business associates, or by appealing to staunch party supporters who share your political convictions. This last group often contributes out of loyalty to the cause you represent, and it is usually a major source of funds.

In fact, one of the best ways to assure adequate financial support is to start a reform movement or a "clean government" crusade prior to announcing your candidacy. Those joining such a movement will usually select the campaign leader as their candidate and contribute both time and money to the cause.

Rosalind Wiener, when in her early twenties, joined a Democratic party organization in Los Angeles and started a clean government crusade. It led to her election to the Los Angeles City Council. With funds supplied by her party supporters, she handed out small bars of soap, dramatizing the theme of her campaign.

Pledge Cards

In utilizing direct mailings to solicit support, candidates frequently enclose pledge cards as a means of building up their campaign organizations. The card often contains a thumbnail-size photo of the candidate printed in the left-hand corner. Alongside of this is a statement to be signed by the voter, pledging support.

On the other side of the card is a brief biography of the candidate, telling where he or she was born, education, family status, business or profession, past political experience if any, qualifications, etc.

Here is the "pledge" side of a sample card:

<table>
<tr>
<td>

</td>
<td>

John J. Smith for County Assessor

    Believing John J. Smith is fitted by ability and experience for the office of County Assessor of _____(name)_____ County, I hereby pledge my support and vote in the ___(date)___ primary and general election and authorize the use of my name as a member of the Smith for Assessor Campaign Committee.

Name _____

Residence _____ Phone _____

City _____ County _____

Party Affiliation _____

</td>
</tr>
</table>

The pledge card may be mailed with your fund-raising letter, or, better yet, some time prior to it, with the brochure or letter that describes yourself and your candidacy (see chapter 14). As the cards are returned, they are filed in alphabetical order for future reference. Those pledging support are called upon to give voluntary assistance during the campaign. Some may help address literature; others may serve on the speaker's bureau or do door-to-door canvassing. Some may prefer just to donate money.

Professional Collecting

In a campaign for an important state or federal office, you will require professional assistance, not only in collecting funds, but in managing and publicizing your candidacy. Today there are many professional campaign organizations that specialize in all of these fields. They will take over the technical functions of the campaign or advise you in setting up your own organization.

One of the first businesses of this kind was started in 1933 in California, when Clem Whitaker, a newspaper reporter, lobbyist, and public relations man, joined with Leone Baxter, a chamber of commerce secretary-publicist, to form Campaigns, Inc. of Sacramento. Its success in handling both Republican and Democratic campaigns led to the creation of other similar organizations. Campaign Associates, Inc. (408 Petroleum Building, Wichita, Kansas) is one of the most widely known associations of this kind. It also publishes a bi-monthly, newsletter-type magazine analyzing current campaigns and reporting on winning techniques and strategies. It is operated by Hank Parkinson, president, and Robert A. Stone, vice-president.

Some professional organizations may be hired by candidates of either (or any) party. Others will work only for Republicans, and still others only for Democrats. Fees for statewide campaigns may range from $30,000 to $50,000. Candidates desiring professional help in running their campaigns may obtain information on consultants in their areas by writing Mrs. Phyllis B. Brotman, President, American Association of Political Consultants, 1101 North Calvert Street, Suite 1406, Baltimore, Maryland 21202.

Professional fund raisers usually operate in pairs. Their procedure frequently follows the formula outlined below. You might want to use some of these techniques yourself.

1. They set up a collection headquarters—something like a "bucket shop" promotion office in a hotel or office building—and have telephones installed.

2. They have impressive stationery printed, showing names of the respected citizens sponsoring the campaign. A fund-raising letter is printed on the stationery and mailed out to their list of potential big money givers.

3. They call all members of the executive committee sponsoring the campaign, asking their aid in putting pressure on prime prospects.

4. They telephone everybody on their list of big money givers to make appointments. This avoids embarrassing delays in getting larger donations.

5. Solicitors are dispatched in pairs to call on prospects. They tactfully suggest the amount which they hope to obtain from the prospect before he himself has named an amount.

Do-It-Yourself Methods

Fortunately, expensive expert help is not needed for conducting an ordinary campaign for city or county office. Enlist as volunteers as many experienced, community fund raisers as possible. Persons who have been soliciting funds for the Red Cross, the Boy Scouts, or any kind of community welfare, can be most helpful.

Several days before sending your solicitors out door-to-door, mail to prospective contributors a brochure or letter that describes the candidate and the platform. If you are doing bulk mailings, mail them out in plenty of time—mail delivery can be slow.

In an industrial area where most of the voters are workers, schedule the fund-solicitation drive soon after the regular pay day. Have your solicitors give each contributor a receipt, thanking the donor.

Obtain the names of the big contributors from your party officials and go after them first. Many executives would rather give money than contribute their time.

For years, $100-a-plate dinners have been used successfully to raise campaign money. They are usually underwritten by a fairly wealthy or well-to-do sponsor, and invitations are sent out to prominent persons of considerable social standing. Often, in addition to the candidate, some prominent party leader or a celebrity is featured as a speaker.

In selecting a celebrity or party leader as a speaker, you must consider the backlash effect on voters. Certain names might help sell tickets for the dinner but would cost you votes because many of the voters in your area were prejudiced against them. For the same reason, holding a cocktail party to raise money may be good in one community, but not in another. In certain strong church-going communities, it could cost you more votes than it would contribute to your campaign fund.

To make fund-raising dinners successful, invitations must be printed and everything carefully arranged. Special prizes are sometimes offered to those buying tickets, but to do anything of this kind, lottery laws governing give-away events must be checked. In some communities even Bingo for charity is prohibited.

The 1974 Campaign Finance Act, which restricts certain expenditures in political campaigns for federal office, permits a sponsor of a dinner, cocktail party, or coffee hour to spend up to $500 in hosting a political gathering of this kind on behalf of a candidate. Provision U.S.C. 431 of the act specifically excludes from the legal definition of campaign expenditures "the use of real or personal property and the cost of invitations, food and beverages" for any such event as long as the total cost of the event does not "exceed $500 with respect to any election." If its cost exceeds $500, it must be counted as a campaign expenditure.

THE FUND-RAISING LETTER

Your fund-raising letter is, obviously, an important part of your fund-raising drive. Its primary function is to raise money, but it also helps sell you and your candidacy. Your hope is that its recipients will be inspired to return a donation to you by mail, but the letter is always followed up by a door-to-door solicitation.

You must make your fund-raising letter appeal to the voters' basic interests. For example, if taxes are a major concern in your area, you will point out how a vote for you will be a step toward tax justice and that any contribution he or she can make will be helpful.

Print the letter on your campaign letterhead stationery. Address the letter specifically to the voter, not to "occupant," if you have the equipment and funds to do it that way. This personal touch always makes the letter more effective.

Here are ten rules for writing the letter:

1. Make your first sentence capture attention.

2. State as convincingly as you can why the major issue of your campaign concerns the voter's pocketbook, health, or family.

3. Provide facts and figures to support your statement and cite specific cases.

4. Point out as convincingly as you can why it is up to the voter to join in the campaign to eliminate the menace, inequity, or problem of concern, and the need for financial assistance.

5. Write plainly and naturally, just as you would speak, being careful to avoid stereotyped, threadbare, or legalistic phrases.

6. Make your letter personal in tone, addressing the voter as a friend and neighbor.

7. Cite names of a few outstanding sponsors and any endorsements that might prove influential.

8. Inject as much enthusiasm into your letter as possible, yet avoid any exaggeration that might cause it to seem insincere.

9. Be sure to request that checks be made payable to your campaign headquarters.

10. Be sure to sign the letter personally, unless it is mass produced and this is impossible.

11. Enclose, if possible, a photo-copy of a newspaper story giving a brief biographical sketch of you and a concise statement of your program.

Add this P.S.: We must have money and volunteers in order to win.

7
Outlining Your Campaign

Although you may have already mentally outlined, at least in skeleton form, the basic strategy of your campaign, your first step in planning your campaign should be to draw up a blueprint. By blueprint, we mean a *written* program or plan of action, including a time schedule for recruiting volunteer workers, making appointments, and conducting the day-to-day work of your campaign. Writing down your work plan, your campaign objectives, and strategies to be employed in achieving those objectives will not only serve as a reminder but will also aid you in formulating a winning program. Writing things down always helps the creative process.

Begin drafting your blueprint by getting a large tablet and making notes in answer to these questions:

1. What is the main objective of my campaign, and the major problems that must be solved in attaining that objective?

2. What are the major concerns of voters in my area that can be translated into winning campaign issues?

3. Which issue should I make the central theme of my campaign in order to win the majority vote?

4. What allies, in the way of newspaper editorial support and endorsements by prominent leaders, can I count on?

5. Can I count on strong party support? If not, from what persons and groups will come my principal aid?

6. Where will my maximum opposition come from? How can I best neutralize this opposition?

7. What are the best ways to publicize the issues? What strategies will best promote my candidacy?

After jotting down tentative answers to these questions, call a council of your most trusted advisers, including your campaign manager if you have selected one, and discuss each question. Since three or four heads are often better than one, such an exchange of ideas is nearly always profitable. Big metropolitan newspapers hold similar huddles every day when their editorial staffs meet to evaluate the news and decide which stories merit the front-page headlines. Merchandising and advertising agencies, likewise, hold brainstorming sessions in developing their sales campaigns.

YOUR INITIAL PUBLICITY BARRAGE

In following the above procedure to determine your campaign strategy, main line of attack, and foreseeable problems, you are doing what generals do in planning a military attack. A general sets a zero-hour when his artillery and bombing planes will begin battering the enemy's defense lines, an attack to be followed up by tanks and infantry. Your initial artillery barrage will be publicity releases, announcing your entry into the campaign, stating clearly why you are filing as a candidate, and issuing a challenge to your opponent on what you consider the key issue of the campaign.

You will later follow up this initial publicity with the announcement of the appointments of campaign manager, campaign chairman, campaign treasurer, and secretary. The opening of your headquarters will also be reported in your early publicity.

In each of these announcements, your publicity must endeavor to present your central campaign theme—the reason you are a candidate and the key issue on which you are running.

GETTING INFLUENTIAL SUPPORTERS

Another of your early releases should list the names of leading, influential citizens endorsing your candidacy. In preparation for this announcement, you should jot down the names of friends, business associates, party officials, business groups, church societies, labor groups, young people's associations, senior citizens' clubs, and ethnic organizations. Checking these lists, you must carefully select the names of key persons who you think will endorse and support you. Some of them may have signed as your sponsors when petitions were circulated to get the necessary signatures of registered voters on your nominating papers. Others on the lists may have signed and returned your pledge cards.

All of these names on the list must be carefully considered before you use them, for you must avoid using any that might embarrass you with the voters. The endorsements that will aid you most are those recognized as leaders—persons of influence and credibility.

Getting the right persons to endorse your candidacy is extremely important, both in getting money and votes, because many persons do not trust themselves to make independent judgments in politics but instead follow leaders. This trait of human nature helps to explain the tremendous power once exercised by big city bosses.

"Folks are a lot like sheep," remarked one city boss, who preferred to remain anonymous. "All you need is a goat to lead the sheep when you're loading them on a railroad boxcar. In politics, you've got to find the right goat to lead the voters."

House-to-house agents selling subscription books in small towns and rural communities have made use of "the flock leader" technique. They launch their community selling campaigns by first getting pastors and civic leaders signed up as purchasers. Then other citizens will fall in line. The late Huey "Kingfish" Long learned this lesson in leadership psychology while selling Orison Swett Marden's books, *Pushing to the Front* and *Every Man a King*. The technique helped him win a seat in the U.S. Senate.

By getting the right "flock leaders" early in your campaign, you have taken a major step toward winning. It is the key to big contributions, and in some industrialized areas, the labor endorsements alone can assure success.

OBTAINING EARLY MEDIA COVERAGE

In drawing up your time schedule, you must plan to do two things early in your campaign:

First, get acquainted with the publishers and editors of your local newspapers, if you don't know them already, and try to enlist their editorial support. If they say they have a rule against making political endorsements, ask them for an even play on campaign news. *Even though you may plan to leave most of the news handling to your publicity director, it is important for you to cultivate a personal, friendly relationship with the working press as well as with publishers and editors.*

Second, sew up choice radio and television time ahead of your rival. In contracting for preferred time for your spot commercials, consider the hours when the voters you wish to reach with a particular commercial will be listening. Community listening habits vary, so check with your local stations as to what is considered preferred time in your locality, or have your publicity director or radio official do it.

PLANNING YOUR CAMPAIGN BLITZ

As you plan your campaign operations and expenditures, jot down the means you will use in getting your message to the voters. These are:

1. Publicity releases and advertising, including newspaper display ads, radio commercials, television spots, direct mail letters and brochures, bumper stickers, posters, and billboards.

2. Personal speaking appearances before various organizations, press conferences, etc. Outline your speaking itinerary.

3. Speaker's bureau. List prospective speakers to enlist for your bureau team.

4. House-to-house canvassing and telephone vote-soliciting.

5. Rallies, special programs, and sound trucks.

In your campaign, it may be necessary to eliminate some of the above, such as television, bumper stickers, or billboards, and to spend more on direct mail and house-to-house distribution of campaign literature. But all of your campaign's promotional effort —speeches, canvassing, and advertising of every kind—must be consistent and coordinated, and it must be aimed at a single objective: your election. That means that your newspaper publicity and paid advertising must call attention to your and your associates' speaking engagements, your rallies, parades, and your house-to-house vote drives. It means following through on precinct weak-spots discovered by your field workers. It means always emphasizing your main theme or slogan, so the public knows you are what you stand for.

Whatever you do, you must not neglect the recruitment of all the free volunteer help available. In a local campaign, it can be one of the most effective factors in winning.

Young persons will often, if asked, take part in a campaign as a volunteer just to get experience and learn more about the democratic process. Don't overlook this source of help. They can be particularly helpful in distributing literature, putting up posters, and house-to-house canvassing.

ORGANIZING GROUP CONTACT WORKERS

Since campaigning is a multi-faceted activity, you will need people to do special contact work with various groups. In a large city, county, or state campaign, you will need a speaker's bureau, and special committees to solicit votes among women's groups, labor, business groups, veterans, first-time voters, senior citizens, home or property owners, mobile home residents, tenants, church groups, nonpartisan or independent voters, professional societies (doctors, teachers), farmers and agricultural groups, and lawyers.

These are some of the usual standard committees needed in a campaign, but in a large state campaign you may also require special committees dealing with ecologists or conservationists, barbers, cosmetologists, apartment house owners, or various tax-concerned organizations. In certain communities you will also need interracial committees or black and Spanish-American divisions.

Each committee should have its chairman or chairwoman and conduct a special drive for votes among its particular group. To enable these committees to function effectively, you must prepare a kit for each member of each committee to use. The kit should contain the following: an explanation of the committee's function; a biographical sketch (giving the candidate's place of birth, education, business or professional career, political experience if any, family status, etc.); *a brief statement telling why your background and experience qualifies you to be the right candidate to represent the special group to which the vote-appeal is being made;* and your platform or stand on important issues involved, along with your pledge to the voters.

If you are the favored candidate of your party, you may not have to organize your own precinct leaders, block captains, canvassers, poll-watchers, etc. These functions are usually performed by regular party workers. But in an important statewide campaign, you should not rely upon party workers. Organize your own. In fact, in most campaigns, the safest policy is not to rely upon your party organization for anything you can do yourself.

YOUR CAMPAIGN TIME SCHEDULE

Using the following outline as a guide, devise a time schedule for your campaign. It outlines the order of business for a November election.

First Phase: May 1 to September 1

1. Announce and publicize your intention to be a candidate. This may discourage certain others who are thinking of running, and reduce the competition.

2. Get your nomination papers signed and filed.

3. Continue planning campaign strategy, and begin recruiting volunteers.

4. Find out what help you can get from your party.

5. Appoint your campaign chairman, manager, publicity director, and treasurer. Publicize the appointments.

6. Continue organizing volunteers, selecting block captains for every block or precinct area where needed to supplement party workers. This is usually done in close cooperation with party officials.

7. Start your circulation of pledge cards and develop your card system, indexing voters. Contract for prime radio time for ad spots.

8. Draw up a tentative budget, based upon estimated costs.

9. Plan and initiate your mass fund-raising drive.

10. Open your campaign headquarters with fanfare and publicity.

11. Organize your contact committees for labor, veterans, etc.

12. Start training members of your speaker's bureau and house-to-house canvassers, supplying them with special kits.

Second Phase: September 1 to October 1

1. Send out thank-you notes to all who rendered special aid in the primary, or thank them by press or radio.

2. Start a new round of speechmaking and canvassing.

3. Step up your personal appearances, press conferences, and interviews. Continue publicity calling for volunteers and stressing your campaign theme.

4. Renew your appeal for funds, using direct mail, solicitors, and advertising (newspaper and radio).

5. Print and distribute your literature, brochures, direct mail leaflets, posters, and bumper stickers.

Third Phase: October 1 to October 20

1. Start holding rallies and parades.

2. Hold pep meetings with staff workers to step up your fund-raising and canvassing drives. Try also for increased publicity by dramatizing the issues of the campaign.

3. Hold daily strategy sessions with your campaign manager and other key campaign advisers.

4. Begin planning a major television speech that you will give on election eve.

Fourth Phase: Two Weeks Before Election

1. Launch extensive telephone solicitation of voters.

2. Begin holding street-corner rallies as a prelude to one major rally just before election. Hire a school band, if possible, and use sound trucks to remind voters of the main issue and your name.

3. Build to a climax with major speeches, interviews, publicity, and advertising (newspaper display ads and radio commercials.)

4. Plan for election day by training poll watchers and checkers. Also arrange for baby-sitters and car-drivers to aid in getting your supporters to the polls.

Fifth Phase: Election Day

1. Some political advisers suggest distributing sample ballots to voters outside of polling places, but this is questionable in some communities. Some states prohibit any form of electioneering in the proximity of the polls.

2. Have your poll watchers and checkers ready to go on duty the moment the polls open. Substitutes should also be available.

3. Dispatch baby-sitters and drivers to places where needed.

4. Have your telephone supporters call voters reminding them to vote.

5. Hold an election-night party for supporters, and make a personal appearance to thank all.

Sixth Phase: Follow-Up

1. Analyze the results to see where you ran strong and where you lost.

2. Send out personal thank-you letters to all who gave substantial aid to your campaign, and use newspaper and radio ads to thank all who voted or worked for you.

3. Keep your campaign records. The name lists, with addresses and telephone numbers, can be very valuable if you plan to run again or decide to aid a friend.

8
Creating a Winning Program and Image

One occasionally hears political pundits on television and radio debating which is more important in winning a campaign: image or issues. The question is about as useful as debating which came first, the chicken or the egg. *Both* a good image and an attractive issue are of prime importance.

It is true that a personable candidate does win now and then despite his issues or program lacking a wide popular appeal. In such a case, his success may be credited to his having charisma— that mysterious quality for working miracles.

You, too, may have charisma, but don't count on it. To play it safe, you must strive to create the most favorable image possible. You must create the image that you can do a better job than your opponent. At the same time you must work to devise a program, emphasizing one or two popular issues that you can use in persuading voters to cast their ballots for you. To be attractive your issues must promise solutions to certain major problems with which the voters are most concerned.

Since first impressions are very important, you must begin projecting a good image and championing the *right side* of a basic issue early in your campaign. Seize the initiative by taking the strong side of a problem of major concern and speaking out on it from the start.

You must never wait to let your opponent define the issues.

If you do, he may choose the winning ones, leaving you without a strong one to champion or putting you on the defensive. In announcing your candidacy, you should state your program and your reason for running as clearly as possible.

YOUR IMAGE

No matter what you promise or how attractive a picture you can paint of the future, you must sell yourself to the voters as one capable of delivering on that promise. To do that selling job effectively, your campaign literature, your endorsements, and your publicity must emphasize your qualifications for the office you seek. The voters will need to be convinced that you have the good judgment and executive ability to do the job, and that you are a person of credibility and responsibility.

Good photographs of yourself and your family for use in your campaign brochures, folders, and posters are an important part of this image-selling job. These photographs should be new and taken from the best possible angle.

If you are a nineteen-year-old candidate, you may find it advisable to dress and wear your hair in a way that makes you look older. If you are near retirement age, you may improve your election prospects by modifying your dress and hair style to create a younger image. But in either case, be careful not to overdo it. There is nothing more pitiful than an oldster dressed like a teenager.

Your reputation for credibility, the way you speak, and the way you smile are all a part of your image. The photograph you use in your campaign literature and your mannerisms when addressing a public meeting or appearing on television are also components of your image. Your speaking habits and mannerisms are important. By consciously paying attention to them, you can improve your image.

During the televised presidential debates of 1976, Ford and Carter were being judged by the viewing audience as much by the images they were projecting as by what they were saying. Ford often appeared too grim. Carter, on the other hand, seemed to belittle the seriousness of certain statements he was making by smiling just as he finished the statement. This mannerism, according to psychologists, may have caused some of his television viewers to have questioned the truth or sincerity of what he was saying, because most persons do not believe a matter of grave concern should be discussed in a light, casual, or smiling manner.

Undoubtedly, the way you speak, shake hands, and greet people on the street are all a part of your image. Smiling, certainly, helps in doing that part of campaigning. Smiling and appearing relaxed will also help make a favorable impression if you are being interviewed on television or making a brief impromptu speech. *But when you start discussing that big issue in your campaign, you must appear deadly serious so as not to give the impression of minimizing its importance.* However, keep your remarks brief and to the point. Don't engage in a lengthy, grim-faced harangue. Close with a promise of victory, and a smile.

The Importance of Belonging

To win the acceptance of voters, especially in a community that has a rather permanent, non-migratory population, you must try to convince them that *you are one of them*—that you belong.

If you've ever talked to people about their voting preferences, you've probably heard some say, "I'm voting for Jimmy (or Johnny) because he's one of us." This tendency of human nature is strong, especially in rural areas where there are few changes in population or life styles. If the voters regard you as an outsider, someone alien to their way of life and their community's traditions and customs, their attitude presents a challenge.

One of the quickest ways to win acceptance, if you are a newcomer, is to join a local church and the community's most active social organizations. The important thing is to get in the action—get yourself known. Join the Rotary, Kiwanis, Lions, or Optimist clubs, and if you are a veteran, join the American Legion, Veterans of Foreign Wars, Amvets, or whatever organization you are eligible to join. Get active in the PTA, Boy or Girl Scouts, Chamber of Commerce, and community improvement associations, and start speaking out on community subjects. Activity of this kind will aid you in quickly identifying with the life of the community.

This is the key to political survival and victory in a new neighborhood. Otherwise, a slightly foreign accent and a manner of attire that doesn't quite conform to the customary attire of the area may cause you problems.

Both accent and colloquial expressions of speech are as important as outward attire in campaigning in certain areas. One old-time Tennessee politician is said to have always put an acorn in his mouth before making a campaign speech to his constituents. It gave his words the right vocal twang, he explained. Abraham Lincoln realized the importance of maintaining his image as a product of the wild frontier. When campaigning among farmers, he pitched hay, cradled wheat, and split rails. Carl Sandburg in his famous book, *Abraham Lincoln: The Prairie Years,* explains that Lincoln did this "to show the gang he was one of 'em."

A Car Can Be Too Shiny

In seeking to identify with the so-called common man, or the average wage-earner, you must dress like him and not drive a Cadillac, or you will damage your image.

When the late Adlai E. Stevenson campaigned for governor of Illinois in 1948, he did his campaigning in a rented Chevy, rather than use a Cadillac offered him free of charge by some of his LaSalle Street friends. This was smart campaign psychology. For in his bid for the governorship, he was seeking the vote of the class-conscious haters of the rich. At the time he was flaying what he called Governor Green's "corrupt, careless and cynical greed machine."

Now that the United States is becoming increasingly energy-conscious and large, gas-guzzling cars have become a target of criticism, the kind of automobile you drive may become politically more potent than ever. The best political advise would probably be "In Rome, do as the Romans do."

BEWARE OF INTERVIEW TRAPS

To be a successful politician, one must learn to be wary of reporters, but never cynical. Much of Richard Nixon's trouble was due to his cynicism about the press. In 1962 when he was defeated by Brown in a campaign for governor of California, he said angrily that the press would have to find someone else "to kick around."

A positive-thinking, less cynical attitude is more conducive toward creating friendly relations with the press and other media, and these good relations are extremely important in building a winning image. Yet the relationship is sometimes an adversary relationship. It is not uncommon for inquiring reporters to ask infuriating, almost insulting questions at press conferences and during television interviews.

Indeed, both new and experienced politicians frequently damage their images by granting television interviews on highly controversial issues. They sometimes become ruffled and angry, seem obviously evasive, or appear to be resorting to double-talk instead of giving a clear, sensible answer to a question. Consequently, television interviews and even press conferences can be dangerous.

In such situations, you must remember to keep calm. If you show anger, you are projecting the wrong image. The trick is to appear relaxed, frank, honest, and unruffled. But that is often very difficult when being prodded with provocative questions. But if you have chosen a politically sound stand on key issues, you should be able to withstand sharp questioning. In fact, these questions may be just what is needed to aid you in clarifying your stand on the issues so that the voters will understand your position and be convinced. If that happens, the interview is a big plus for your campaign.

By replying in a straight-forward manner, under hard questioning, you also create confidence in your ability. Voters prefer candidates who tell them plainly and frankly where they stand on the issues. Failing to take a definite stand is usually regarded as a sign of weakness in position or lack of moral courage.

IMAGE ALONE IS SELDOM ENOUGH

Your grasp of the issues is at least as equally important as your image. When Ronald Reagan ran successfully against Edmund G. (Pat) Brown for governor of California in 1966, the Spencer-Roberts team handling his campaign shielded him from newspaper reporters. His campaign managers were convinced that Reagan, an experienced public speaker, projected a much better image on television. Worried about Reagan's television effectiveness and the fact that he was a handsome ex-movie actor, Brown, then sixty-one, sought to improve his own physical image. He began dieting and exercising daily and reduced his weight by twenty pounds. But he did not improve his speaking ability or his grasp of the key issues, and he went down before the more articulate Reagan.

In chapter 2, we mentioned the remarkable achievement of the Fort Worth radio flour salesman, Wilbert Lee O'Daniel, who won election as governor of Texas in 1938, although he was opposed by thirteen of the best-known Democrats in that state. Moreover, O'Daniel had spent much of his adult life in Kansas and had no southern drawl, and he was only a recent convert to the Democratic party, then the ruling power in Texas. Indeed, his radio broadcasts as a biscuit-flour salesman had made him widely known throughout the state, but he certainly did not seem to have the right image to win in Texas in 1938.

Although some have attributed his surprise victory to a combination of clever politics and showmanship, featuring hill-billy music and the hymn-singing zeal of an old-fashioned religious revival, what is generally overlooked was the wide appeal of his program. He promised a change—a businesslike administration. In addition, he denounced the professional politicians, and he promised a $30-a-month pension for the elderly as a forerunner of social security.

His program compensated or made up for what he appeared to lack in image. It was based on issues of wide appeal.

YOUR PROGRAM

In creating an election-winning program, you face a problem similar to that of a sales manager concocting a successful sales plan. He begins by studying the merchandise, carefully researching what the buying public wants, and then considering the selling points of his merchandise. He asks himself how these selling points will appeal to different groups of prospective buyers: housewives, businessmen, etc. In other words, he analyzes the basic appeals that his product will have for different types of persons.

That is the way you must consider your image and your vote appeal in formulating a winning program.

Using the research techniques outlined in chapter 5 for finding the main issues or the problems of major concern to the voters in your area, select several of the leading ones to include in your program. If you are running as a party candidate, you will be expected to choose issues coinciding with those endorsed in the party platform. Yet most successful candidates place the emphasis upon one or more key issues of their own choosing. Hayakawa did that in winning his senatorial seat in California in 1976.

For instance, in a campaign for mayor or city council, you might combine issues such as these into an economical crime reduction program: (1) restructuring the police department to provide more efficient patrolling, quicker police response in emergencies, assignment of more policemen and policewomen to high crime areas, and the use of more decoy, undercover officers; (2) formation of a citizens' block-watch organizations using CB radios to co-operate with law enforcement agencies in crime prevention; and (3) organization of a city commission to work with various civic, religious, and social groups to reduce juvenile delinquency by providing better recreational facilities for the young.

If you are a candidate for judge, you might combine the following issues into a juvenile delinquency program: (1) the need for new laws so that juveniles who commit murder and other serious crimes of violence will be treated as adults; (2) the need for less judicial leniency for habitual offenders; and (3) the need for improved facilities and rehabilitation programs for juvenile offenders.

That, of course, is a hard-nosed approach to the problem, but if juvenile crime continues to increase at the rate it has from 1970 to 1977, some communities will support such a program.

In a campaign for mayor or city council, one might create a winning program by combining the following issues: (1) better street lighting to reduce crime and accidents, (2) a more efficient mass transportation system, and (3) a modern paramedic emergency service, operated by the fire department.

But whatever you promise in your program, it must be stated

in more concrete and specific terms than some of those nebulous promises of the past that are still unfulfilled. In other words, you must try to make it believable and convincing.

Those Unsolved Problems

When running for his first term in Congress in 1946, Richard Nixon set forth six points in his program which would be his aims if elected. They were adequate housing for all, lower taxes, veterans' rights, full production with lower prices, freedom for the farmer, a new labor policy.

Consider these for a moment. How many of these problems have been solved? Certainly, Nixon is not the only one to blame if these problems are still with us today. Congress and other presidents must share the blame. Various attempts toward tax relief have been made, but when county officials promise not to raise taxes, they simply raise the assessment valuations.

Instead of "adequate housing for all," we have a national housing dilemma—a situation where many young couples are unable to buy homes because of inflationary building costs and because most of the money being loaned at high interest rates for residential construction is going to $40,000 and $50,000 homes, which is above the young couple's price range.

Many of the old problems are still with us. They just have new faces. Some have grown larger with the years. This means there is still plenty of opportunity for energetic young men and women who can devise new, creative solutions to these political problems and put them into execution.

Street crime, school vandalism, unemployment, inflation, inadequate housing, the energy shortage, and the need for conservation of our natural resources are all going to continue to be vital issues in many communities for some time to come. They challenge all of us. They continue to cry for solutions.

Back in 1944, Sidney Hillman, head of the CIO Political Action Committee, was saying:

> After the war is won, we are for:
> A job for everyone who wants work—
> Fair wages for every worker—
> The protection of the rights of labor in every possible way—

The protection of the small farmer—
A good home for every family—
Medical care for all who need it—
A chance for everyone to become educated—
All help to the returned soldier until he establishes himself in civilian life—
Enough insurance for the sick, the aged, the unemployed, the crippled, the widowed and the orphaned—
Fair play with all the nations of the world.
In that way, you can help build a better America for yourself, for your children, and for the common people.

It would seem to be difficult to find anything seriously wrong with that idealistic picture. Yet in many respects, it is still only a dream. In fact, it reads much like what Jimmy Carter was saying in 1976, at least in a general way, doesn't it?

Utopia may still be a long way off, but some progress is being made. You are sure to find some unsolved problems to include in your program. Try to find those of major concern in your area. But you must be specific—attack specific issues with specific solutions. Voters want to hear more than a litany of unsolved problems —they want to hear your solutions and how you expect to execute them. Your solutions must seem realistic and effective.

And remember that a smile will add political magic to your image.

9
Planning Attack Strategy

Let us assume your political opponent, a member of the city school board, has voted to award a large school building contract to a firm in which he is a silent partner, and you discover his business connection. If you are a political realist and serious about winning, you will call attention to this "conflict of interest" deal.

Or, perhaps, your opponent is a member of the city council and he has voted to authorize the city's purchase of a certain tract of undeveloped land for a park, and investigation reveals he is a member of the company owning the land. This, of course, makes him fair game for political attack.

If you are congressionally ambitious, you may discover that your district representative has accepted money or free air transportation from a wealthy foreign businessman or has voted himself and fellow Congressmen a pay raise, while at the same time voting for a reduction in veterans' pensions or welfare. It requires little imagination to see how this can be developed into a serious political attack.

But there are many ways in which you can attack a political opponent even if he is not so openly vulnerable. This chapter will point out the various kinds of attacks that can be made and the most effective ways of using them.

ARE ATTACKS NECESSARY?

You may protest that you do not wish to attack your adversary, and that you will wage a purely constructive campaign on your own merits. Most of us at sometime have heard a candidate say, "If there's any mud-slinging or hate-mongering in this campaign, I won't be the one doing it."

No smart politician will recommend either "mud-slinging" or "hate-mongering." A well-documented attack or exposé based on truth is something else. It is essential.

Professor William Bennett Munro, teacher of political science and governmental affairs at Harvard and other American universities, offered one of the best explanations of why the attack is an essential part of every successful campaign. He said, "People vote their resentment, not their appreciation. The average man does not vote *for* something, but *against* something."

Most practical politicians operate on that theory. They know that it is easier and more effective to stir people up and get them angry so they will vote against some candidate or program than it is to inspire them to vote for a good candidate and a promising program.

In fact, nearly every candidate needs a whipping boy—that is, someone to be made the target of the voter's wrath, or something generally believed responsible for a bad situation. A newcomer in politics may make "the Professional Politician" his whipping boy and try to put his opponent in that category. In 1948, President Truman made "the do-nothing Congress" his whipping boy in his famous "give 'em hell" campaign. During the 1939–1950 period when Americans were much concerned about the communist menace, the "Secret Card Carrier of the Red Conspiracy" became the whipping boy in several campaigns.

Cries of "Professional Politician" and "Watergate Connection" were still politically damning in 1976, and some candidates have lost in fairly recent elections for being "Members of the Establishment." It has been advantageous in some political races to be "An Outsider."

It is the ammunition used to "throw the rascals out" or "clean up the government" that makes the difference between fair campaigning and "mud-slinging," although the difference may occasionally be blurred by semantics.

Regardless of how factual and carefully documented your attack may be, your opponent will probably try to dismiss it as a smear concocted of lies, innuendoes, and distortions. Don't let that upset you.

ATTACK SUGGESTIONS

1. Center your main attack on your opponent's official record or lack of qualifications.

2. Carefully avoid attacking your opponent's personal or private life, especially any marital difficulties. In chapter 4, it was pointed out how Democrat Gary Familian lost to Robert K. Dornan in a 1976 California contest for Congress because Familian made this kind of mistake, along with others. Since alcoholism is now widely regarded as a disease, this would also be dangerous as an attack charge unless your opponent's alcoholism has resulted in injury to the public or caused his arrest on a charge of drunk driving. Even then the charge might be politically dangerous unless he has been declared guilty.

3. Always make certain that any attack you make on your rival can be legally and convincingly documented.

4. *Take care not to attack an opponent on anything that might create sympathy for him and win him votes as a consequence.* For instance, you would not attack him for having been a member of the Ku Klux Klan in a community where many voters were once KKK members; nor would you attack him for being a member of the Jewish Defense League in a predominantly Jewish community. To attack him as having been a member of the John Birch Society in an ultraconservative community might be equally dangerous. In a liberal voting community this line of attack could be helpful.

5. Any criminal conviction in a candidate's background makes him vulnerable, unless many of the voters feel he has been completely rehabilitated and deserves another chance. Then bringing up his criminal record could create sympathy for him.

6. If he has written a book or any published article that can

be construed as un-American, antisocial, or subversive, it may be the basis of an attack.

7. Association with persons of questionable reputation is frequently made the basis of attack, but "guilty by association" was given a bad name and discredited during the end of the McCarthy era. It is still used, however.

8. If you can prove that your opponent is a member of a corrupt political machine and guilty of "cronyism," that is, showing special favoritism, you may have dynamic attack ammunition.

9. Fashions in attack change, but never attack any candidate, male or female, for being too old. In 1976 John Tunney referred to the age of his seventy-year-old opponent, Dr. Hayakawa, and lost his U.S. Senate seat. Sympathetic senior citizens do not permit this reflection on gray hairs to go unchallenged.

10. To question a young man's ability because of his youthfulness or a woman's because of her sex could prove equally disastrous. Not only would such criticism generate sympathy for those in their age or sex groups, but it could also spark a backlash vote by Americans who believe in fair play. References to race, sex, and religion are also out of bounds in political campaigning.

Having made a thorough investigation of your opponent's record and background, as suggested in chapter 4, you have undoubtedly found some basis for an attack. Is it important enough to use? Or is it something so trivial that it will be readily discounted as "nit-picking"? Unless it seems important enough to influence voters, don't use it.

The "Red Label"

One of the most hazardous lines of attack that a candidate can make on an adversary today is that he has a subversive background, or at sometime was a communist card carrier, or in some way aided an alleged communist conspiracy. But in 1950, Richard Nixon and his campaign director Murray Chotiner defeated Helen Gahagan Douglas, who was vying with Nixon for a U.S. Senate seat, by charging that during her five years in Congress she had voted 353 times exactly in line with New York Congressman

Vito Marcantonio, then widely known as a follower of the communist party line.

Chotiner did not voice the charge himself. It was made public in the campaign by Bernard Brennan, chairman of the Nixon campaign committee. Nixon echoed the same line of attack and said that after the election he would force Mrs. Douglas to "tell where she stands."

The "Red Label" attack played a key role in her defeat, although she had supported various anticommunist measures and had been denounced by the Soviet press as a "capitalist warmonger." Actually, Marcantonio, who had originally run for office on the Republican ticket although he was a member of the American Labor Party, had often voted with the Democratic majority on uncontroversial matters of no major importance. So this contrived effort to smear Mrs. Douglas as pro-communist appeared to be an unfair distortion of her position. Although this charge undoubtedly was effective at the time, Nixon was to be haunted by it during the remainder of his political life.

Chotiner, for a time, continued to use a similar technique in other campaigns, but criticism arising from its use in the Douglas defeat and the subsequent emphasis given the communist menace by Senator Joe McCarthy eventually brought it into discredit as a proper line of attack. Paul M. Butler, chairman of the Democratic National Committee at the time, accused Nixon of trying to ride to power on un-Americanism as his basic issue. And when Joe McCarthy began to point a finger at members of the Eisenhower administration, he was rebuked by the Senate for unfair investigative tactics. Both Republican and Democratic leaders indicated that charges of un-Americanism were taboo. Consequently, this particular line of political attack appears to have virtually disappeared.

WHO WILL MAKE THE ATTACK?

Many professional campaign strategists, including the late Murray Chotiner, have suggested that much of the main attack directed at an adversary should not be made by the challenger, but by a third party. Often the candidate, who piously foreswears mud-slinging, may not make the attack personally, but leaves the attack, especially if he expects serious backfire, to his allies, a special campaign committee, or a political columnist or commentator. Sometimes this facet of the attack job is assigned to a "professional dynamiter," or a team of hatchet-men operating under the name "committee of concerned citizens."

Actually, this form of indirect or covert attack from a supposedly neutral corner is often more effective than a frontal attack by the challenger himself. It may carry more weight with the voters because it does not appear to be personally motivated. It is not new. Charles Michelson, publicist and "unofficial ghost of the Democratic Party" in the 1930s, tells in his book, *The Ghost Talks,* how he used committees of this kind to attack President Herbert Hoover.

In Los Angeles, Jim Mellen, a self-proclaimed "President of the Jeffersonian Democrats" during the 1930–1950 period, assisted Republican candidates in defeating Democrats for state and national offices. In his radio broadcasts, Mellen often flayed the Democratic candidates much more viciously than his Republican associates would have dared to, since they did not wish to risk the possible backlash. Mellen was known in local political circles as a "political dynamiter." Through his aid, Republicans often defeated Democrats in districts with predominant Democratic registration.

During the 1976 presidential election, Ford was subjected to this form of oblique attack when a government agency leaked reports to the news media about an investigation of his possible misuse of campaign finances during his prior congressional campaigns. Finally the governmental inquiry ended with the belated report that nothing illegal had been uncovered, but by that time, many voters may have been influenced by the suspicion created.

The intervention of committees, of course, can be beneficial to the democratic process if they tend to focus attention on important, meaningful issues at a time when opposing candidates, locked in a name-calling controversy, are actually neglecting the main issues.

While the indirect form of attacking a rival may work well in a campaign for high office, it is not so useful in the average campaign for a low-level office. In the ordinary campaign for city council, school board, or sheriff, one of your prime needs is personal publicity—and by personally making the charges against your opponent, you get favorable newspaper and radio publicity. This is especially true if you are a newcomer running against an incumbent who has the probable advantage of being better known.

You can often increase the effectiveness of the do-it-yourself campaign attack by leaking some of the information of an incumbent's wrong-doing or weakness as a candidate to a friendly newspaper and letting the press publish the initial exposure as its own. That can open up the issue for public discussion, providing a favorable prelude for your entry as a champion for a cleanup. It also helps to establish the newspaper as an ally in your campaign. The main danger in doing this, provided your information is true and well documented, is that your adversary's principal weakness or wrong-doing may be published too far in advance of the campaign. The voters may cool on the issue and interest may dissipate by election day.

TIMING IS IMPORTANT

In timing your attacks, you must try to have a blockbuster for release just before election, so that your opponent will not have time to answer it adequately or offer a satisfactory alibi. Planning the attack strategy of a campaign is something like writing a suspense story. Something big and emotionally moving has to be held back for the climax. You must not shoot all of your fireworks too soon.

UTILIZING YOUR SPEAKER'S BUREAU

Your speaker's bureau can be especially useful in helping you press your attack on particular weaknesses of your opponent. If, for instance, he has shown himself to be anti-labor, the speaker who represents you before labor groups can point these facts out at meetings of union members. In a campaign for judge, members of your lawyers' committee should be able to enlist cooperation in talks with county or state bar associations and with the local organization of trial attorneys. In other words, members of your speaker's bureau can present the lines of attack that will appeal to the concerns of the particular audience at hand.

A FINAL WORD

One final word of warning: always try to attack your opponent on his weak points, not on his strong ones, unless you can convincingly show them to be wrong. For example, it would be an error to attack your opponent for having strong consumer rapport, unless you were in some unusual place where consumerism is a bad word. During the 1976 presidential campaign, Ford criticized Carter for showing so much interest in consumerism and for conferring with Ralph Nader. Ford, who had never shown himself to be a staunch supporter of consumer rights, obviously did not realize that millions of Americans are consumer conscious and also respect Nader for his contributions to consumer protection. This remark by Ford, undoubtedly, cost him votes.

Summing it up: experience points out that you will probably have to attack your opponent in order to win, but that you must make certain your attack is based upon facts that can be documented. Your attack must be fair and so timed as to swing the votes in your favor on election day. If all of your attacks are timed too early, your campaign may peak before the climactic day.

10
Dramatizing the Issue

You must try to find a way to dramatize the key issue in your campaign and a trademark or symbol that will make you stand out from other candidates. For one of the key techniques for winning in politics, as in almost every other field of leadership, is to capture the imagination of the people, achieve identity as an individual, and incite enthusiasm for your cause. To quote Napoleon: "Imagination rules the world."

How do you do this?

DON'T JUST TELL—SHOW!

One of the most effective ways of capturing the imagination of the voters and winning favor for your cause is by using showmanship to make your message clear, vivid, graphic, and persuasive. In other words, you must dramatize the basic issues in such a way that the voters are aroused to what the issues mean to them in terms of their own self-interest. Actually, you are following the advice of the drama teacher who tells student writers, "Don't tell it. Show it in action."

Howard Metzenbaum dramatized the economic breadbasket issues in Ohio during his successful 1976 campaign for the United States Senate by campaigning with a loaf of bread and a box of cereal under his arm. He used them to dramatize what inflation was doing to American food prices.

Running for city council in Los Angeles, Rosalind Wiener, a twenty-year-old Democrat, handed out small cakes of soap to dramatize her campaign theme—a cleanup of city government. She won.

Hayakawa used an appeal to the voters' imagination in winning election to the United States Senate from California in 1976. He wore his tam-o'-shanter to remind voters of a dramatic moment in California history, when he—wearing the tam-o'-shanter that became his trademark—had defied student revolutionaries at San Francisco University in 1968. He also used imagination effectively when he dramatized his opponent Tunney as a playboy by a clever television commercial. It showed a young man, resembling Tunney, skiing down an icy mountain while a seat in the U.S. Senate remained empty.

G. Lynn Sumner in his book, *Meet Abraham Lincoln,* tells how Richard J. Oglesby of Decatur, Illinois, a friend of Lincoln and a man of considerable theatrical ability, conceived the idea of dramatizing Lincoln as "The Rail-Splitter."

In 1860, the Illinois Republicans were planning to hold their state convention in Oglesby's home town. Seeking some way to spotlight Lincoln's appeal to local citizens, Oglesby learned that in his youth Lincoln had split rails in a nearby community. Lincoln's rail-splitting partner, John Hanks, still lived there. Oglesby looked up Hanks and found that some of the old rail fence which Lincoln and Hanks had made in 1830 was still in use. Oglesby tied two of the rails to his buggy, brought them to town, and hid them in his barn.

When the state convention got under way a week later, Oglesby stood up and announced that a former Democrat wished to make a contribution. Old John Hanks climbed upon the platform, carrying the two rails that he and Lincoln had split in 1830. On the rails was a sign stating: "Abraham Lincoln Rail-Splitter, Candidate For President In 1860."

Loud applause rocked the convention hall, and the convention went on record endorsing Lincoln. From then on, John Hanks and his rails were a regular feature of Lincoln rallies, and "Abe

Lincoln, the Rail-Splitter" won adoption as the campaign slogan. When the Republican national convention was held in Chicago in May, 1860, Lincoln was nominated for the presidency, although political writers had expected Seward to be the nominee.

To the philosopher, there is a thread of irony in this. Lincoln, probably the most uncommon man in American history, was elected president because the common man thought he was one of them. If he had been portrayed as a genius, a great thinker who would write a classic speech like the Gettysburg Address that would live for all time as an example of eloquence, they very likely would have rejected him. Dramatized as "the rail-splitter" and one of them, he won.

In a like manner, Jimmy Carter won as "the peanut farmer from Plains, Georgia." If he had campaigned as a nuclear scientist and smart businessman, he would not have done so well, because the American voter likes to identify with and feel a kinship for the man he chooses to represent him in public office.

Dramatizing is effective in identifying you and selling your campaign issues to the voter. As Dale Carnegie once wisely observed in his best-selling book, *How to Win Friends and Influence People,* "Too much talk is tiresome. It is ineffective. People like action, dramatic action." Carnegie added, "This is the day of dramatization. Merely stating a truth isn't enough. The truth has to be made vivid, interesting, dramatic. You have to use showmanship. The movies do it. So does the radio. And you'll have to do it if you want attention."

Dramatized ideas reach the great mass of voters who do not react to more subtle political reasoning.

In his book, *Political Behavior,* written some fifty years ago, Frank R. Kent pointed out the need of using showmanship in presenting campaign issues. He wrote: "Give them a really good show and they will warm to you, rally around you, support you. At bottom, what they want is to be amused, not instructed. The thing they abhor is to be bored. Actually, except in times of industrial depression and unemployment or when some national crisis impends, it is a difficult thing to get the voters really aroused over any issue. Constructive proposals as a rule leave them cold."

Political human nature hasn't changed much over the years, although television and other techniques of reaching voters have.

The appeal you wish to make and the type of voter you wish to reach will determine the kind of dramatization you use. For example, Malcolm Wallop used an unusual television commercial in Wyoming in 1976 to defeat Senator Gale W. McGee. McGee, a Democrat with a strong following, had served in the Senate since 1958. Since he was aiming his campaign against Washington bureaucracy, Wallop decided to dramatize this by ridiculing various bureaucratic restrictions imposed on ranchers. So he concocted a television commercial action-shot of a cowboy taking a portable toilet with him as he started out to do his daily stint on the open range. It not only got laughs but emphasized a point.

Another of Wallop's commercials showed a person adding more and more postage to a letter. This was an indirect thrust at McGee, who was chairman of the Senate Post Office and Civil Service Committee. Because many Wyoming residents, especially ranching and farm voters living on the plains, resented Washington regulations that seemed to impinge unnecessarily on their lives, these television commercials won favor for Wallop's antibureaucratic campaign. Newspaper reporters credited the television spots with playing an important role in Wallop's victory. A native of New York and a Republican, his chances of winning against a veteran Democrat incumbent had not looked promising at the beginning. His victory was another one in which dramatization made the difference.

HOW YOU MIGHT DO IT

Let us assume that you are a candidate for city council in a city where property taxes have become almost unbearable, and you are advocating economy in city government to reduce the tax burden. How can you dramatize the issue?

You might do it with a television commercial showing an elderly couple answering the door bell to be met by an official who has come to notify them that they are being evicted—that their home had been sold to satisfy a property tax bill. A voice would then say, "You, too, may lose your home if this heavy, extravagant spending continues. Stop it! Vote for Janie Smith for city council."

If street crime is a problem in your city and you are running on a crime reduction program based on more night police patrols or improved lighting, you can dramatize the issue this way. An elderly man is looking out the front window of his home and is saying to his wife, "I'd like to go for a walk in the park like I used to, but I don't dare to." A voice says, "Let's make Jonesville a safe place to live. Vote for Jim Brown and his anti-crime program."

These ideas may not be applicable to what you have in mind, but they can serve as springboards for your creative thinking on how to dramatize your campaign program. So ask yourself "How can I present my campaign theme most graphically and convincingly?"

Many television studios, radio offices, and advertising agencies have skilled, imaginative specialists to help you do just that. But be wary of ideas that are zany and too far-out. Some of the voter reaction they generate is quite different from what was intended.

There are many ways of dramatizing issues besides using commercial spots on television and radio. For example, you may use billboards or ads with a graphic, punchy message, challenge your opponent to a debate, get supporters to stage a demonstration, or enlist the aid of a friendly newspaper in publishing an exposé focusing attention on an important campaign issue.

HOW OTHERS HAVE DONE IT

A Red-Hot News Item

While making his first race for the U.S. Senate following his appointment by Governor Earl Warren, Senator William F. Knowland became a target for criticism from the left because he had spoken out against sharing the atomic bomb secret with the Soviet Union. A radical group supporting Knowland's Democratic opponent, Will Rogers, Jr., was urging that the United States share its nuclear know-how with Russia.

During the heat of this controversy in 1946, William Z. Foster, head of the American Communist Party, came to Los Angeles. Speaking to a group of comrades one night, Foster told them that he had come to California to help defeat Knowland. Reporter

Walter L. Scratch, later editor of the *Hollywood Citizen-News,* had succeeded in getting into the meeting unnoticed. He realized the news value of Foster's statement and showed a copy of his story to the newspaper's publisher, Judge Harlan G. Palmer.

"Call Knowland and tell him what we are running," Palmer said. Scratch did as directed. Knowland promptly ordered numerous copies. In many of his campaign speeches that fall, Knowland mentioned that the communists had made him a target for defeat and would then read the *Citizen-News* report of Foster's declaration as proof of the fact. The communist party leader Foster had unwittingly dramatized an issue that helped elect Knowland to the Senate.

This incident illustrates how a political enemy can sometimes become very helpful in dramatizing your candidacy and your program.

The Lumber Scandal

In the same 1946 campaign, Knowland also made another enemy who contributed in a major way to his success. Knowland learned through Carl Greenberg, political editor of the *Los Angeles Examiner,* that the War Production Board had granted Tony Cornero a permit for lumber to rebuild Cornero's gambling boat, then anchored a few miles off Long Beach. This was at a time when veterans who had recently returned from World War II were living in chicken coops and shacks of various kinds in Los Angeles and Long Beach because they were unable to get lumber for homebuilding, since it was then under government control due to scarcity.

Knowland lashed out at the War Production Board's policy, declaring that homes for veterans should be given priority over rebuilding a gambling ship. Veterans and other groups immediately adopted resolutions supporting Knowland's stand. The *Examiner* published photos of the huge piles of lumber stacked ready and waiting for the rebuilding of Cornero's ship, and also photos of the shacks in which veterans were living.

Cornero, goaded into fury by the unfavorable publicity that his gambling ship was receiving in the *Examiner* and other newspapers that had joined in the controversy, struck back at Knowland in a two-column tirade published in the *Los Angeles Daily News.*

At the height of the controversy, a coop in which one veteran and his family were living caught fire. The veteran was burned to death. This created additional sympathy for the veterans' housing plight and rallied more support for Knowland's stand.

To make sure that Knowland got maximum benefit from this issue, dramatized by controversy and a death attributed in part to poor housing, the Knowland campaign organization distributed photocopies of the news articles, including Cornero's attack on Knowland, to religious and veterans' groups throughout southern California. Knowland said he had never intended to pick on Cornero, that his concern was in seeing that the nation's returning war veterans got fair treatment.

There is a good lesson in political campaigning in both the Cornero and Foster episodes. They point up how a hated, feared, or unpopular enemy can be one of your greatest assets in dramatizing an issue and inciting a favorable emotional reaction.

How a Letter Cost an Election

Occasionally a letter, a debate, a suit for libel, or an exciting exposé of some kind will spark fire into a campaign. In 1888, President Grover Cleveland was running for re-election and was locked in a contest with Republican Benjamin Harrison. The Republicans were trying vainly to make an issue out of the Ceveland administration's free-trade policy that favored Great Britain, but most newspapers and the voting public seem uninterested. But one letter dramatized the free trade issue and stirred lazy minds into action.

One autumn night, George Osgoodsby, a farmer and amateur politician living in Pomona, California, wrote a letter to Lord Sackville-West, the British ambassador to the United States. Osgoodsby signed the letter "C. F. Murchison," and represented himself to be a young Englishman, seeking advice on how to vote in the presidential campaign. Lord Sackville-West replied, advising him to vote for Cleveland. Osgoodsby quickly turned over the ambassador's letter to the *Los Angeles Times* publisher, Colonel Harrison Gray Otis, a Republican leader. Otis published it and wired copies to New York and Washington dailies. The news that the British ambassador was recommending a vote for Cleveland became an immediate national sensation, resulting in a senatorial investigation and the defeat of Cleveland, who received 168 electoral votes to Harrison's 233.

Marcantonio's Show

Although Vito Marcantonio of New York has now passed from the political scene, there are many who still remember his graphic, attention-getting showmanship, his demonstrations, and his radical ideas that won him election and re-election to Congress.

In his 1948 campaign for re-election, he displayed a huge sign on a two-story building in Manhattan's upper Fifth Avenue. The sign read: "Don't pay rent increases. If your landlord asks you for a rent increase, report here and I shall help you fight the Real Estate Trust. Your Congressman Vito Marcantonio."

At that time many of his political enemies believed that his record of consistent support of the communist line in Congress would be enough to defeat him, but the sallow little Congressman created a new show with which to dramatize his appeal to the slum-ridden areas that constituted his stronghold.

On his nightly campaign sorties, Marcantonio took with him a ventriloquist, dressed in high hat and fashionable evening clothes, and a dummy similarly attired. The ventriloquist was introduced as "Mr. Wall Street" and the dummy as "Social Register."

Denouncing the capitalists for their plots against the working people, Marcantonio would wave a copy of the Social Register at the close of his act and ask, "Do you want the Four Hundred to represent you? Or do you want me, one of the 140 million working Americans?"

With these theatrics, Marcantonio won again for the seventh time. For the thousands of uneducated and underprivileged persons in the district, he had dramatized the issue as a choice between a working man, who would safeguard their interests, and a capitalistic dummy, who would betray them to the money interests.

You, too, can probably use a ventriloquist and a dummy to dramatize an issue in your campaign for Congress, or a place on the city council or your local school board. The idea has many possible applications. The gullible are forever waiting for a young David the Giant Killer to come and save them from the professional politicians, the trusts, Wall Street, or, in modern times, the Establishment.

THEATRICS, YES — CLOWNING, NO

Huey Long, with his flashy, bright-colored pajamas and his vocabulary of colorful invectives, knew the value of the spectacular. He also knew how to dramatize himself as the champion of the common people. His success as "The King Fish" was proof of the verity of Frank Kent's theory that the average voter often wants to be amused more than he wants to be instructed.

Unfortunately, there are too many clowns in politics. But the lesson is clear. *To win, you must get attention and arouse emotional concern. One of the most effective ways of doing that is by dramatizing your message—the significant issue—to clarify it and make it vivid and appealing. That is how you get a following.* Cold logic and abstract discussions cannot do that.

EQUAL TIME

If your opponent is an incumbent and is getting free news coverage on TV, you can demand equal time. Whether you get it or not will depend upon the FCC, if the network or station giving the incumbent free news exposure rejects your petition. The "Equal Time" law, section 315 of the Federal Communications Act, came under fire in 1976 and may be changed at any time. In 1976, Senator George McGovern and other minority party candidates for president were barred from taking part in the final presidential debates between Ford and Carter. This resulted in protests. The rules have been changed considerably since the "Equal Time" act was first written in 1934.

For instance, Congress has amended it to exempt a candidate on a news program from the equal time requirement. However, it has been the practice of the FCC to permit a reasonable discussion of conflicting viewpoints. The problem of complete fairness to opposing candidates remains unsolved. So if you feel you are being unfairly treated, appeal to the FCC. You may not get justice, as you see it, but you could get some publicity. A complaint, publicized in the press, that you are being treated unfairly might result in voters' sympathy.

RADIO, A POWERFUL ALLY

For many years radio has been one of the most powerful mediums in American politics for reaching and influencing voters. This fact has been demonstrated repeatedly in both local and national campaigns.

Several years ago, the Radio Advertising Bureau conducted a nationwide survey. It indicated that 92 percent of the women in the United States listen to radio—housewives listen as much as sixteen hours and forty-six minutes every week. Men were estimated by this study to be listening to radio more than fourteeen hours a week.

While television has cut in on radio's listening time, six million radios have been sold in the U.S. since the survey. Often a housewife or a worker in some form of business or trade can listen to radio while doing their tasks, duties they could not perform while watching TV. Millions of American men and women also listen to their radios while commuting to and from work daily. The blind, many of the nation's elderly, and persons living in remote areas that do not have television are all a part of the tremendous radio audience.

Regardless of what kind of an office you are seeking, local or national, you must devise a way to use the full potential of radio in your campaign. Since radio time is much less expensive than television, you should try to utilize it to the maximum in your campaign. Your first step is to compile a list of radio stations and to make contact with their news and advertising departments.

Nearly all AM radio stations broadcast news frequently during the day, some every half hour. If you can get your advertising plugs inserted along with newscasts, you can reach a large listening audience. And if your campaign generates some "real news," the local radio stations will usually carry it as news free of charge.

Of course, you will have to pay for the broadcasting of announcements and endorsements. In buying radio time, as in contracting for TV spots, you must try to get periods when the listening audience is largest, or when the particular voters you wish to reach will most likely be listening. The best spots are usually between 7 a.m. and 9 a.m. and between 5 p.m. and 6 p.m., if you are trying to take advantage of the favorite news broadcasts. These are the best hours in many metropolitan communities because commuters are driving to and from work at that time. Spots just immediately before popular talk shows are also good.

Capitalizing on Radio Talk Shows

One way to benefit from talk shows is for you or your campaign workers to telephone the talk show personality and ask questions about timely issues, particularly those involved in your campaign. Often questions of this nature will spark the talk show operator into a lively discussion. You or your campaign spokesmen can then steer the discussion into a channel that will aid your candidacy and the issues you are championing.

If you are advocating some kind of a consumer reform, this tactic should not be too difficult, since most radio and television

PLANNING YOUR PHOTOGRAPHS

Good photographs are important. The photos that you use in your publicity should be planned with the deliberate purpose of catching the eye of the newspaper reader and assuring a favorable reaction. In other words, your photos should be planned to appeal not only to the editor, but to your constituents. A smiling expression is usually good, but it must be used with discretion. For instance, if your photo is to be used with a news story in which you are condemning some governmental policy or injustice, a smiling photograph would not be appropriate. It would seem incongruous. The facial expression in the photo should fit the story.

While a mug shot of you looking toward the camera is okay, a full-length photo of you staring straight at the camera is often objectionable because it appears stilted. An amateur will often make the mistake of looking at the camera instead of at a gift or a scroll when being presented with one. A photo of you bending over gracefully to hand a little girl or an elderly lady a flower is often good for a campaign pose. Or you could be pinning a medal on a Boy Scout. Presenting a certificate or a small award to a teenager for writing a prize-winning essay on a reform issue highlighted by your campaign is another photo idea.

Photos of you shaking hands with persons of political prominence, especially with those endorsing your candidacy or program, will be helpful. During the primary, a photo of you with the party county chairman should aid.

Editors of daily newspapers with staff photographers often prefer to take their own pictures. Your publicist can assist in arranging for them to do this, setting up the scene and notifying the press when and where the photos can be taken. Occasionally, a newspaper will suggest that you come to the office to be photographed. Always comply, if you can. News cameramen are often temperamental and have rather definite ideas about what kind of poses they want, especially in taking action shots. Try to go along with their ideas.

Action in a photo can, of course, be simulated. You can be photographed gesturing or pointing, as if making a speech. If you have won some local renown as a football player, you could be

photographed crouching or ready for a kick-off. A kick-off picture would be a natural for use with your announcement that you are a candidate.

If you are a candidate for a local office, ask the Sunday editor of the largest daily in your area if he would like to have a member of his staff do a special article about you and your favorite hobby, at the time you are announcing your candidacy. Regardless of whether your hobby is gardening, collecting rare stones, tossing horse shoes, or painting, this can probably be developed into an interesting article. It will aid you in gaining local recognition.

Special Uses of News Photos

One particular use of photographs in a campaign needs emphasis. It is *telling the story of your campaign* as it progresses.

You can start your photographic story with an action shot of you at the clerk's office filing your nomination papers. You can also start with a picture of you holding aloft a sheet of paper, as you issue a challenge to your opponent or announce your candidacy. Follow up with photos showing you shaking hands with the governor or some other person of prominence who is congratulating you on your decision to run. Another may portray you wearing a hard-hat and overalls as you address a labor meeting.

In case you are campaigning in a dairying region, you can do as Gerald Ford did in his first campaign for Congress—have a photo taken of you milking a cow. Or you can crown the community's dairy queen. In a farming region, you can be photographed visiting a farm that has distinguished itself in some manner, or discussing agricultural problems with farm leaders. All kinds of action shots that tell a story can be used in publicity. These can be hoeing your garden, washing the family car, typing one of your campaign speeches, enjoying a picnic dinner with your family, playing croquet or pitching horseshoes with some elder citizens.

Give some thought to how you can devise a series of news events of pictorial interest. Often newspapers will send out staff photographers if you can set up an interesting scene.

Photographs can also be used to rebut an attack by your opponent. For instance, if you have been made the target of a vicious

attack, you can make light of it by getting a photo of you standing under an umbrella. You can caption the picture: "Neither wind nor rain nor his opponent's mud-slinging can stop candidate Smith's campaign."

Some Photos Do More Harm Than Good

Photo press-agentry, however, sometimes goes awry. Early in his career, Big "Kissin' Jim" Folsom of Alabama found baby-kissing to be a good publicity gimmick, and the smiling, lovable governor gave the traditional stunt a new twist. He started kissing "babes," teenaged and older, as well as the babies. From Texas to California, he bussed beauties. The news cameramen never tired of shooting pictures of Big Jim doing his thing. It seemed to be working like political magic until a young woman sued Folsom, alleging that he was the father of her child. At that point, the governor decided kissing was no longer beneficial to his campaign, and he stopped the practice.

Folsom's experience demonstrates that even baby-kissing has its hazards as a campaign technique, and that a candidate has to be careful in using photographic publicity. Two Los Angeles County Superior Court judges also discovered this fact several years ago when running for election. Their publicity man, who was schooled in Hollywood press-agentry, arranged to have them photographed on a miniature golf course. Convinced that "cheese cake" or "leg art" was a favorite with newspapers, he decided to have the two male jurists attired in Prince Albert coats and colorful under-shorts, showing their bare legs. This unusual leg display, he was sure, would please the editors.

Sure enough, the editors used his grotesque photographs of the judges, who customarily wore black robes while on duty to enhance their dignity. The publicist was jubilant, but the public was shocked. So also were their fellow jurists and members of the Los Angeles Bar Association. It was an affront to the dignity of the court and the justice system, some said. Both jurists were subsequently defeated.

Having your picture made with the "wrong people" can also be politically dangerous at times.

GETTING THE WORD TO POLITICAL EDITORS AND OTHERS

As a candidate in a community campaign, your main newspaper contacts will often be with political and city editors. In a state or federal campaign, publicity releases and wire dispatches covering political news may be handled by state editors and foreign (non-local) news editors. However, in a local campaign, you and your publicist should not confine your contacts solely to the city and political editors. The women's page editor, the society editor, and the sports editor may all be helpful in getting your campaign publicity before the readers.

If some phase of your campaign is of special interest to women, or if you have an important women's group working in your campaign, news releases should be directed occasionally to the editor of the women's page. For example, if you are scheduled to speak before a women's club meeting, advance publicity should be given the women's page editor.

If you are being honored in some sporting event or are making an award to some local athlete, your news release should go to the sports editor.

If the newspaper has a columnist who frequently comments on political affairs, contribute some items concerning your candidacy. Editorial page writers usually resent having a candidate send them editorial suggestions, but if you know one well enough, you may enlist his or her aid in promoting interest in the major issue of your campaign. Your name will not have to be mentioned, as long as your key issue is given a boost.

Your newspaper publicity, if it contains live news, will frequently be picked up by television and radio news commentators, since their news staffs usually rely heavily upon the daily news for news tips. The three big national television networks, for instance, get much of their early morning news from the *New York Times* and the *Washington Post*. However, your publicist must not count on the local television and radio news staffs picking up your stories from the newspapers. Their news editors should be on your list to receive publicity releases.

PRESS CONFERENCES

In the larger metropolitan areas, press conferences have become a popular and effective way of releasing important statements in a political campaign. To set up one, the publicist mails out notices to editors or phones them inviting them to send reporters.

Another way to get maximum newspaper coverage of an important announcement during the course of your campaign is to have your publicist phone the editors *on the day of the meeting* and invite them to send reporters. To assist reporters, the publicist prepares a statement explaining the purpose of the meeting and some direct quotations.

If you set up a press conference, *be sure to be prepared to answer questions, be on time, and be certain that the announcement you intend to make is important and real live news. Otherwise, your press conference can be a failure.*

A press conference may not be the best way to make an announcement if there are certain subjects in the campaign that you do not wish to discuss publicly at the time, or if you feel uncertain about your ability to skillfully parry some of the questions the reporters may ask (see "Beware of Interview Traps," in chapter 8). A press release may be a better way to make the announcement.

CAMPAIGN TOUR PUBLICITY

When starting out on a county or state campaign speaking tour, publicity releases giving your itinerary, along with information as to time and place of speaking engagements, should be given newspapers in the area to be covered. Take with you typed portions of the speeches covering those particular points you wish to get published. This will help prevent your being misquoted.

Before releasing a statement or report of a speech for statewide distribution, it is often advisable to phone the Associated Press or UPI service bureau manager informing him that you are sending the copy by special messenger. Mark it "Rush" and check to see that it is delivered to the bureau without delay.

You will have a better chance to get your story on the wire if

you have a good, strong, compelling direct quote in your lead sentence. To use this news form, you put the "what" element—what was said or done—first. An example:

> "It would be folly for the United States to continue to downgrade solar energy, while spending billions on nuclear power plant development since the problem of disposing of radioactive waste is still unsolved," George Smith, candidate for Congress in the 15th district, declared last night before a crowd of 300 persons.

That puts the punch of what was said up front. And that is important in getting political speeches published. Try always to make your leads as newsy and interesting as possible.

THE CLIPPING FILE

Effective use of the press entails keeping track of how—how frequently and in what light—you are represented in it. Thus a newspaper clipping service is a necessity in any campaign for high office, and very useful in any kind of a campaign. In a small city or school board election, you or a member of your staff can clip them for filing. Nearly all professional publicists maintain an up-to-date clipping file. They need it to see how well their publicity is doing and to keep informed on that of your opponent. Unfortunately, most clipping services do not deliver the clips until the end of the month. To keep currently informed, you should have a member of your staff read and clip your local newspapers every day.

13
Getting the Most out of Radio and Television

Television has completely changed political campaigning for high state and federal offices in America, and radio continues to be a powerful medium for reaching and influencing voters in both high and low-level campaigns. But many candidates fail to make the most effective use of either television or radio. To do that they need expert assistance. Here are a few basic rules:

1. If you are running for a minor office in a small town or rural community, spend your money on radio and other low-cost mediums for reaching the voters, instead of on television spots.

2. If you are seeking a high state or federal office, spend as much as you possibly can on television.

3. Choose the television or radio station that can give you the best or nearest prime time for reaching the particular type audience you desire—the one that is right for you.

4. You can reach more women on daytime radio from 8 a.m. until about 6 p.m.

5. Your best time for reaching the farm vote is in the early morning when farmers listen to farm prices and special farm programs, and at noon in some communities.

6. Your best buy in television time is in 20-, 30-, or 40-second or 1-minute commercial spots between two 30-minute popular programs.

TV OR NOT TV

There can be no question about the important role that television plays in presidential and other high-level campaigns. It's use can be decisive. The reason television is so politically potent in a state or national campaign is that it enables the candidate to come into the voters' living rooms and talk to them intimately. Through it, he can present himself and his issues more vividly and convincingly, with lifelike realism, than through any other medium.

But television is definitely not the best medium for minor campaigns. There are three main reasons why this is true. First, television is very expensive, and the money it would cost you in a minor campaign could be more effectively spent on radio, newspaper advertising, and house-to-house contact work.

Second, through radio you can reach more voters in your community. This is especially true in rural areas. While less than 300 metropolitan communities in the United States are served by local television, more than 2,000 have radio stations. There are more radios in cars in America than television sets in homes.

Third, successful television campaigning, interviews, and personal speaking appearances require special skills. While short spot announcements and graphic commercials can be very effective, some candidates actually lose votes by appearing on television. On television, you are in competition with talented, highly skilled commentators and the nation's leading politicians.

In the smaller campaign where you can get around and shake hands with your constituents and talk with them as a neighbor about the problems that most concern them, television isn't necessary. Such close, personal contact is much more effective.

MASTERING EFFECTIVE SPEAKING SKILLS

Television is the newest medium for mass communication during campaigns, and many candidates have not yet mastered the speaking skills needed to project an attractive, persuasive image.

For example, during the 1976 presidential campaign, Gerald Ford often spoke on television in an old-fashioned, oratorical style as if he were addressing a county fair. His speaking style in

1977 seemed to have improved. Carter in 1976 erred in a different way. He often spoke too quietly and indistinctly and sometimes seemed to disparage or deprecate a serious statement he had just made by smiling. Many other candidates, however, do far worse, some delivering long, tiresome tirades in rasping, raucous tones. Some speak too glibly and too fast.

Of course, effective, persuasive speaking skills must be used on both television and radio. Here are several ways to practice and improve your skills:

1. Practice speaking before a mirror and record what you say. Then play the recording back, and listen to yourself. Using a tape recorder this way will be very helpful to you in developing a good radio and television style of your own. As you play your speech back, listen carefully and critically. How was your articulation, your emphasis on important points in your speech? Did you speak too fast or fail to enunciate clearly? Did you start a sentence at a high pitch, then let your voice drop or stretch out a word at the end of the sentence? If you notice yourself making speech errors of this kind, a voice coach may help you correct them.

2. Take a course in public speaking or go to a voice coach if you have a speaking problem that needs correction.

3. Make a practice of reading aloud, looking up the proper pronunciation of any word about which you are uncertain.

4. Listen critically to important politicians speaking on television and radio. Notice how they emphasize certain points. Ronald Reagan is an example of a political speaker who has acquired superb skill as a TV and radio speaker through years of practice. He was a radio broadcaster before becoming a film star.

Most politicians practice speech improvement. They also learn to avoid words that they have difficulty pronouncing. Such practice will be helpful to you, even if you are running for a minor office and do not have to use television.

While a voice coach can be of great help to some candidates who have a special speaking problem, any coaching that causes your voice to sound affected or artificial is bad. *In order to be a convincing speaker, you must speak naturally to convey sincerity.*

Old-fashioned, oratorical stump-speaking is not right for either television or radio today. The intimate, conversational tone is the more appropriate style. But you must articulate clearly without slurring words. These are the keys to developing a more effective radio and television personality.

SHORT TV SPOTS

Althought the president of the United States or a governor who has something very important to say may be able to hold the attention of a TV audience during a 30-minute speech, few political candidates can. The attention span of the average TV viewer is limited, and he may also be annoyed because his favorite program has been canceled in order to make time for the speech. A 15-minute speech would probably get a better audience reception, but 15-minute spots during the peak listening hour are seldom available. If you can get one, you are lucky.

Recent research has revealed that these brief TV commercials are usually more productive and efficient than longer ones because listeners turn off the longer ones. The viewing audience for a 30-minute political speech was found to be about one-third of that for the program replaced. Between 5 and 10 percent turned off 15-minute political broadcasts, while tests indicated 60-second TV commercials showed no audience loss.

Because obtaining prime time, or the best time for you to reach the right voters, is so important, you should start buying your spots early. If you cannot get a 15-minute spot, you should try to get some one-minute or 30-second spots between two 30-minute programs.

Television spot commercials are especially good in selling a candidate's stand on issues, and some candidates have found them useful in building a favorable image. One recent case comes to mind. Finding himself fighting for his political life in Indiana in 1976, Democratic Senator Vance Hartke accused his opponent 44-year-old Republican Richard G. Lugar, former mayor of Indianapolis, of using television spots to "sell himself like Fruit Loops, complete with pretty packaging and sugar coating." Lugar smiled and kept on with his image buildup on TV and won.

In New Mexico in 1976, Republican Harrison H. Schmitt, a

former astronaut, and the twelfth man to walk on the moon, used a television and radio blitz to beat incumbent Democratic Senator Joseph M. Montoya. Orrin Hatch, a 42-year-old Salt Lake lawyer, who described himself as "a free-enterprise conservative," also used radio and television effectively to unseat Democrat Frank E. Moss, 65, a three-term senator.

Short TV spot action-scenes, picturing an idea, have been used successfully in many recent campaigns. Senator William Proxmire of Wisconsin has used them to keep his image before the voters. Some of them featured him jogging.

Using TV to Highlight Issues

If water and air pollution are issues in your campaign, you can have an action shot made of you pointing to a major source of pollution—a factory smoke stack belching black fumes of poisonous gases into the air, or a plant discharging chemically dangerous waste products into a lake or river. The major issues in your campaign can usually be pictured in some form. Doing it effectively will call for an exercise of your creative imagination. Inspection of a nuclear power plant, which has become a source of controversy because it is near a quake fault, might also be used as a picture location. By using a scenic background indentifiable with the campaign issue, you add realism to your argument.

The point to remember is *have your TV films made at the proper locales to emphasize the issues of your campaign. This adds credibility.*

Producing the Spot

Creating a good 30- or 20-second spot is often more difficult than concocting a 15- or 30-minute TV commercial because you have to condense a message into such a brief time. Consequently, these very short spots require a different treatment. Often they can do little more than name the candidate, show someone endorsing him or her, and ask for a vote for the candidate. A 15- or 30-minute period gives you much more leeway in winning the voters' support without any hard-sell tactics. A shot of you addressing a group of your supporters at a coffee get-together might even be carried as news.

You should produce both your television and radio transcrip-

tions before you launch your campaign, if possible. One of the most economical ways to make your film is to get a friend who is proficient as a cameraman to shoot a number of action pictures of you, your family, and endorsers with a good movie camera. But if you have the necessary campaign funds, it is safer to employ professional photographers to do the job. This, however, is usually expensive. After the films are shot, you can go over them, edit them, and have them made into short TV news spots.

Since you want your films to show you in the best possible way, your attire is important. A suit of medium color is much better than one that is too light or too dark. A light blue shirt will also photograph well. Women candidates should be careful not to wear heavy lipstick or excessive jewelry, since anything that distracts the viewer from what you are saying or doing may injure your TV image. By all means, try to act natural and speak without affectation. The more informal the setting the better.

If you have marveled at how well big-name politicians are able to orate in easy, almost flawless grammar and quote statistics without seeming to refer to notes, the explanation is very simple. Many of them are using a video prompter, a device that scans typed text and projects it to glass reflectors so the speaker can read it while looking straight at the television audience. Using a prompter, you, too, can make a television speech without referring to visible notes. Of course, you'll need no aid of this kind in broadcasting over radio, but you must be careful not to ruffle your papers too loudly.

TV INTERVIEWS

Interviews, panel shows, and debates can all be used to project you and your program to the public, but all three can be risky because of unanticipated audience reaction. You should carefully consider the problems and dangers involved before agreeing to participate in any of these. If you consent to a TV interview, be sure you are well prepared. Try to anticipate all of the questions that you may be asked, and how you can best answer them. (See also "Beware of Interview Traps" in chapter 8 and "Handling Hecklers" in chapter 11.)

THE IMPORTANCE OF PERSONAL CONTACT

There is one central core of your campaigning that cannot be done by publicity, workers, computers, or television. It is the responsibility of selling yourself—your own personality—to the voters. *They want to know you, shake your hand, look you in the eye, and decide for themselves if they can trust you to manage their political affairs.*

This is especially necessary in campaigning for a minor office in a small town or rural area, but it is important in every type of campaigning. And it is one of the basic ways in which selling a candidate and his program differs from selling detergent.

Your real character and your program may seem intangible and nebulous to the voters. It is not like a box of detergent they can pick up and open. But by touching your hand, looking you in the eye, they feel they are making contact with the real you, and it is up to you to make your program as graphic, real, and convincing as you can.

In campaigning, you are waging psychological warfare. It is more subtle than commercial salesmanship and calls for more refined techniques than those required for merchandising a sales commodity. Occasionally a candidate, impressed with the miracles of Madison Avenue and modern sales advertising, does not comprehend the difference. So he employs an advertising agency that has won distinction in commercial exploitation to handle his campaign publicity and promotion. This can be fatal.

Governor Thomas Dewey's unsuccessful campaign to unseat President Truman in 1948 provides a good example of what happens when an advertising agency's policy for selling detergent is relied upon to sell a candidate. Dewey's strategists decided to depend almost exclusively upon a constructive selling campaign. So they gave him a build up, carefully avoiding controversy, and repeated over and over, ad nauseam, the theme of unity.

Dewey's colorless campaign, which should have been aggressive and challenging, was eclipsed by Truman's rip-roaring, meet-the-people, "Give 'em Hell, Harry" train show. Truman's attack, focused mainly on a convenient target, "the do-nothing Congress," got the newspaper headlines. The result was a surprise victory for

Truman. At least it was a surprise to many of the newspaper publishers, who had endorsed Dewey.

It all proved once again that selling a political candidate to the voters is not like selling detergent. Perhaps, as in waging war, one can be too cautious and conservative to win.

HEART APPEAL IS POTENT

Newspaper columnist Malcolm Bingay may have put his finger on the truth when he wrote thirty some years ago: "The trouble with logical, hard-headed people who know business and government is that, by their very temperament, they do not get aroused. They are content merely to sneer at the crackpots and call them nuts. That is no answer to their arguments."

Bingay went on to point out that in order to sell a political idea you should have the zeal of a "Coin Harvey," the zealous advocate of a two-metal coin standard and the Liberal party's candidate for president in 1931. Flaming crusaders, Bingay said, were needed to preserve the democratic principles of Jefferson and Lincoln—and they are needed now.

Certainly zeal is a prime ingredient in selling a political idea. Unless you can get angry about some public injustice or wasteful, inefficient practice and generate righteous indignation, you are lacking one of the prime requisites for winning success in the political arena. Zeal is needed to defeat the smooth, overly confident incumbent or the rival who is relying mainly on a big campaign fund and strong party backing to win his election.

In selling an idea, the emotionalism of a zealot is often more persuasive than the most brilliant but calmly presented logic. But zeal can go too far. An analysis of Adolf Hitler's success in leading the German people into the debacle of World War II, despite the warnings of intellectuals, points to the truth of this. "If you wish the sympathy of broad masses," he wrote in *Mein Kampf,* "then you must tell them the crudest and most stupid things."

There are politicians in the United States who campaign on that cynical principle, but most Americans are becoming too literate, too intelligent, and too well-informed to be continually misled by liars and charlatans. Those who do win elections by lying and false promises eventually reap the consequences.

But you must aim at the voters' hearts as well as their heads. While the old style oratorical, rabble-rousing approach is out of date in most parts of the country, you must find ways to stir people. You must get them angry and disgusted with someone or something. The sad truth is the intellectual appeal seldom wins, unless presented with attention-getting salesmanship.

THE POWER OF PLAIN SPEAKING

Just plain talk that inspires confidence and makes a point is invariably more effective than flamboyant oratory that has the ring of insincerity. Voters are often suspicious of the candidate who is too glib and too polished. Our motion pictures with their slow, hesitant, almost tongue-tied heroes have tended to foster this suspicion, for the villain is often the glib one.

Many a candidate has lost a campaign because he spoke too rapidly and failed to enunciate clearly enough for his audience to understand what he was saying. If the candidate had only slowed down, used plain words, and spoken with more deliberate emphasis, he might have won. Max Rafferty, a prominent California educator, made that mistake in running against Democrat Alan Cranston for the U.S. Senate in 1968. Several of Rafferty's Republican supporters complained that he spoke too fast—that it was difficult to understand him or follow his line of thought. Cranston, a former International News foreign correspondent and author, spoke clearly and to the point. He won.

When President William McKinley found himself seriously challenged by the Democratic nominee, William Jennings Bryan, one of the nation's leading orators, he did not attempt to compete oratorically. Instead McKinley's campaign manager, Marcus Alonzo Hanna, recruited a "truth battalion" of several hundred forceful but plain speakers and sent them out to follow Bryan's trail. It was a long, arduous campaign trail, for Bryan traveled more than 18,000 miles by train and made more than 600 speeches to five million persons. But McKinley won by 7,104,799 votes to Bryan's 6,502,925. Plain talk triumphed over oratory.

There is a lesson for you in the historic Bryan-McKinley campaign, regardless of whether you are running for city council or governor. It is this: if your opponent is an orator or exceptionally glib, clever speaker, use the plain-speaker technique against him. Question the credibility of hot-air merchants and political windbags who make wild and implausible statements and promises—without naming your opponent. Insist that you do not belong to that school of professional politicians, but that you are going to speak plainly and tell it like it is.

You may question your opponent's more extravagant statements and promises, or you may leave part of this job to your speaker's bureau. But throughout the campaign, you must continue to question his credibility. Your speakers may make pointed references to him that you yourself could not make without generating some possible backlash.

John F. Kennedy realized the wisdom of courtesy in this respect. He would go out of his way to avoid making what might be construed as a malicious comment about an adversary. To say personally uncomplimentary things about a rival is often poor strategy. It is often more effective to have those attacks made by someone else.

VOTERS EXPECT CONSISTENCY

Voters expect you, as a candidate, to be consistent. They expect your statements and the campaign promises made in your advertising to be consistent. If you, as a candidate for city council, promise in your campaign speeches to work for a new mass transportation system or some other costly city improvement, while your posters and newspaper display ads pledge you to an alluring reduction of city taxes, the voters are going to expect an explanation. "How," they ask, "can we have these expensive improvements and also lower taxes?"

If you cannot explain the obvious inconsistency, you are in trouble. While running for president in 1976, Carter encountered a problem of this kind. In some speeches, he had outlined his program for expensive new social services and a strong national defense. In others, he had called for tax justice, including tax rebates for millions of taxpayers. This led some voters to question the consistency of his program. However, he was able to explain these apparently conflicting objectives to the satisfaction of a majority of the nation's voters, thus assuring his election.

Most candidates for public office walk a somewhat similar tight-rope in their campaign promotion. It is one of the challenges of being a candidate. The candidate for city school board faces it when he tries to promise higher salaries to complaining school teachers and lower school taxes to disgruntled property owners. The successful candidate usually tries to avoid making impossible promises, recalling, as someone has said, that "politics is the art of the possible."

HANDLING HECKLERS

In making campaign speeches or participating in radio or TV discussions, you may find yourself a target for needling questions or hostile heckling. What is the best way to cope with them?

A team of University of Missouri behavior specialists recently made a study of this by conducting several tests. According to their findings, audience reaction was found to favor those speakers "who refuted the various criticisms made by the verbal assailant in a calm, friendly and courteous tone of voice and tried to establish good relations with his assailant." The angry retort had the opposite effect.

So the best advice would appear to be *play it cool* with hecklers. You need to respond in the same way you would to prodding, provocative questions, that is, you must appear relaxed, honest, and unruffled.

SLIPS OF THE TONGUE

Often one slip of the tongue or a single sentence can alter the course of a campaign. Many instances can be cited. One classic example is Senator Barry Goldwater's "I would remind you that extremism in the defense of liberty is no vice." He made this unfortunate statement during his Republican convention speech at San Francisco, July 16, 1964. Prior to the convention, fellow Republicans opposing his nomination had been criticizing his hawkish policies for dealing with the Vietnamese war as examples of "extremism." His phrase was quickly picked up by the Democrats and it became a potent key in symbolizing their portrayal of him as a dangerous, trigger-happy leader, who if elected president would plunge the United States into war with the Soviet Union or China. This portrayal of Goldwater led to his defeat by Lyndon B. Johnson.

Gerald Ford goofed disastrously during his 1976 debate with Carter when he said that Poland, Czechoslovakia, and other communist bloc nations were not dominated by the Soviet Union. This remark undoubtedly played a significant role in his defeat. Ford made his indefensible statement so positively at the time that it was virtually impossible to undo the harm through any kind of retraction or explanation. It alienated large segments of the Polish and Slovak voters in the United States.

Carter was also embarrassed in 1976 by his statement about the desirability of maintaining "ethnic purity" in residential neighborhoods. His critics saw in this an implication that whites had a right to seal themselves off from black integration, and vice versa. And while it became a subject of considerable media discussion for a few days, Carter managed to curtail the controversy by explaining that it was simply a "poor choice of words" on his part.

Although the cases cited above occurred in presidential campaigns, a tricky phrase or a "poor choice of words"—often something said in jest or anger—can prove equally disastrous in a campaign for city council or a place on the local school board. The wise candidate keeps his cool. He doesn't say things in anger that may cost him votes later, and he doesn't joke publicly about serious matters. There is always the danger he may be misunderstood.

YOUR SLOGAN

Just as one bad or poorly worded phrase may ruin your chances of winning, a well-chosen slogan, one that is catchy and that symbolizes a key theme in your campaign, may help you win. In 1952, Dwight D. Eisenhower came up with one sentence that brought him millions of votes. It was "I will go to Korea."

It implied that, if elected, he would personally go to Korea and exert all of the powers of his office as commander-in-chief of the United States' military forces to see that this costly war was terminated. He made good on his promise. Not all presidents have been so successful in carrying out the promises implied by their slogans.

In 1916, Woodrow Wilson won re-election based to a considerable extent on the campaign slogan, "He kept us out of war." But soon after taking office for his second term he was forced to declare war on Germany. Herbert Hoover's Republican campaign strategists likewise coined a campaign slogan that later became embarrassing. It was "Two chickens in every pot, two cars in every garage." When the worldwide depression of the 1930s reached the United States and soup lines grew steadily in the big cities, the G.O.P. slogan became a mockery.

In the hard-fought McKinley-Bryan campaign, McKinley's crew of plain-talking speakers sold American voters on the idea that the Republican Party was "the party of business" and that McKinley's re-election was necessary to the maintenance of national prosperity. The label stuck. But times change, and in 1977, Ronald Reagan, California's former governor and one of the acknowledged leaders of the Republican Party, told a G.O.P. strategy meeting that the label "the party of business" had jinxed the Republicans and they should get rid of it. It is no longer true, he said.

How do the voters in your area regard your party? That is one of the factors you must take into consideration in selling your program to the voters. Think it over. Whether you are a Republican or a Democrat, you may find it advisable to seek a new or modified party label.

The lesson for the campaigner is clear. You may coin a catchy phrase that will help you win, but if the promise it symbolizes turns sour, it can cost you re-election later.

Of course, "Throw the rascals out" and "A new broom sweeps clean" have become outworn clichés. You need something newer, like Jimmy Chapman's "Elect a voice for the future" or Rosalind Wiener's "Let's clean the smog away from city hall."

Whatever your slogan, it must be emphasized in all facets of your campaign activity. By repeating the same slogan in all of your advertising and publicity, you cause it to register in the voter's mind along with your name.

PUBLICIZE YOUR SPEECHES ... AND LISTEN
TO YOUR PUBLIC

You can more than double the vote-getting power of your speaking engagements by (1) giving your speeches advance publicity in every medium you can, (2) taking literature—folders, brochures, leaflets, or photocopies of new stories—to distribute at the meetings, and (3) arranging, if you can, to have your speech covered by a news reporter or your publicity person so that you get follow-up publicity.

The advance publicity will not only assure greater attendance and prevent you from wasting time with small audiences, it will also help to keep your name before the voters. The follow-up reports will convey part of your message to voters who were not at the meeting.

By listening closely to what your friends and opponents are saying, you keep in tune with the current public opinion. Also keep alert to what is taking place daily in your campaign and what your opponent is saying and doing. Listen to his radio speeches and read those that are reported. Keep up on all political developments that may affect your campaign.

Hold frequent councils with your campaign aides and ask your trusted advisers whether they can think of any way in which you can improve your showmanship, publicity, and organized effort.

14
Folders and Posters—
Your Campaign Ammunition

In the average campaign, especially one for lower office, the campaign folder or brochure is your most important piece of literature. Distributed by house-to-house workers and mailed out to voters by the thousands, it is the most universally used medium in city, county, and state campaigns. It is one of the prime factors in selling you and your candidacy to the public.

Since it is so important in putting you and your program before the electorate in a favorable light and inducing voters to cast their ballots for you, your brochure should be as good as you can make it. That means it must be graphic, attention-getting, and clearly and convincingly written. It must state your stand on the basic issues in simple, easy-to-understand words. The folder must convincingly point out to the voter how he will be serving his own self-interest in voting for you.

A conventional folder is more effective than one that is too novel. The public has come to understand and expect a fairly familiar format, so too much novelty could detract from your message. It should contain a good, clean-cut facial photograph of the candidate on the front cover with his or her name in big, bold type. The photograph should be a pleasing one chosen with care, for this folder is designed to do a selling job. Usually the word "Elect" or "Re-Elect" appears just above the candidate's name.

Also included in the folder, usually on inside pages, is biographical data telling in concise form who the candidate is; his or her past political or civic achievements; war record, if any; and a statement of the candidate's pledge if elected, along with his program.

Since your brochure is going to serve as your main sales piece, you must concentrate on what goes in it. Don't just dash off a few lines of copy and leave the job of putting it together entirely to your publicity person or printer.

YOUR PHOTOGRAPHS

The photo of yourself that you select for the front cover should be the very best you can have made, and it must be taken from the right angle. You may photograph better with your face turned slightly toward the right or left. A tilted chin may make you appear a bit autocratic. Have several shots made, and pick the one for your folder carefully. Unless you have a winning smile, one that is natural and sincere, a serious, good-natured expression might be better. Certainly, a grim, frowning expression would not be right.

For several years it has been customary to include one or more human-interest photographs of the candidate and his or her family, if any. Often formal family photographs are used, but more casual pictures showing the candidate and members of the family reading or playing together can be used to enliven the brochure. Pictures of this type tend to humanize the candidate in the eyes of the voters and help them identify with you.

Photographs of you participating in some sport or hobby that is popular with your fellow citizens will also aid in this way. It will make the voters feel you are one of them. This sense of belonging as a neighbor and comrade is helpful in campaigning.

If you are a young man fortunate enough to have a wife and baby, their photographs may aid you in getting votes. But if you are a young married woman, a picture of your husband and baby may not be helpful. The baby's picture might inspire your opponent to start a whispering campaign that rather than running for office, you should stay home and take care of the little one. (This line of attack was used unsuccessfully against Sandra Hoeh, whose campaign is described in chapter 20.) Occasionally baby pictures do help. Richard M. Nixon used a photo of himself, his wife Pat, and his first-born in his first California congressional campaign in 1946.

Instead of photos showing the candidate and family, action shots portraying the candidate discussing issues with constituents are often used. One photo may show the candidate talking with a hard-hat worker at a construction site, another discussing an agricultural problem with a farmer. Or the candidate could be photographed conferring with a working mother about the need for day-care nurseries.

Another type of photo that can be used effectively in the folder is one of the candidate with a popular public official or influential person in the community. Candidates running for Congress frequently have themselves photographed with the governor of their state, if the governor is of their party. Endorsement photos are useful in all kinds of publicity—folders, direct mail, posters, and newspaper ads.

SIZE AND STYLE OF BROCHURES

What size should a folder be? What color of paper and ink should be used? Printers and campaign technicians frequently debate these questions. The business envelope-size folder is the most practical and economical for both mailing and house-to-house distribution. Large, expensive brochures, often the favorite of printers, not only cost more, but suggest a big-money campaign. That can be detrimental because it suggests that the candidate is trying to buy his or her way into office.

In one 1976 congressional campaign in California, a businessman spent $171,598, of which $80,000 was his own money, in an unsuccessful campaign to defeat an incumbent, who spent $87,451. One of the mistakes of the businessman was that he put much of his campaign money into very expensive, oversize brochures. They were typographic and lithographic works of art, but the large photographs of the businessman were a waste of money, since he was not particularly photogenic. And his barrage of expensive brochures cast a dark shadow of big money over his campaign effort.

Cases such as this offer proof that a modest, inexpensive brochure may be as effective as a costly, flamboyant example of the printer's art. Yet eager politicians frequently spend campaign money recklessly on garish, oversize pieces of campaign literature. These brochures create an adverse campaign image, just as does driving a Cadillac or Rolls Royce in a low-income district.

A campaign folder must be designed to get attention, but it must not be too arty or garish because it has to do *more* than just get attention. It has to get across your message to the voter. Its psychological effect on the voter must be given primary consideration.

Since name identification is a must in campaign advertising of all kinds, your name should be printed on the front of the folder in large bold type. Often the candidate's name is printed in red, although the rest of the folder may be printed in blue or black. The reason for printing the name in red is that the color stands out and the name registers better in the voter's memory.

As to the color of paper and ink for the rest of the folder, that is a debatable issue. Dark blue ink on white paper is the general preference. A dark colored paper is definitely not good because it makes reading difficult except under a strong light.

For some time scientists have been testing the psychological effect of different colors, and some day campaign folders may be planned with color effects in mind. Red is believed to be one of the most exciting, green and blue more relaxing. So for an inflammatory, revolutionary campaign, a candidate might be expected to use red ink, while an incumbent hoping to relax his constituents might use green or blue. But dark blue ink on white paper is always a safe bet.

Dr. S. I. Hayakawa, the professor of semantics who won a seat in the Senate in a hard-fought campaign in California in 1976, began his campaign with an unusual folder. It was printed in black and green ink on an egg-yolk yellow paper. But the folder was easy to read and was attractively designed. Being on yellow paper, a color rarely used in California campaigns, it got attention. In his folder he briefly and clearly stated his stand on employment, national defense, crime, agriculture, energy, environment, federal bureaucracy, foreign affairs, detente, inflation, and school busing—all highly controversial issues. Yet he handled them all cleverly without stirring a lot of antagonism.

Actually, it is usually considered politically hazardous to state your opinion on a lot of diverse issues in your campaign folder. In the average campaign, especially for lower office, it is safer and more effective to concentrate on the two or three basic issues in which your community is primarily interested.

It is also a mistake to try to crowd too much information into a small folder. Very small type is bad. The trick is to make your message simple and easy to read. Use frequent paragraphs and short sentences.

THE DIRECT-MAIL LETTER

Unlike the mass media appeal or hand outs of brochures, direct mail permits you to make a more personalized, individual vote solicitation. Your direct mail appeal should be like a personal letter asking the voter to vote for you. It should tell him as concisely and persuasively as possible why it will be in his interest to do so.

The direct mail letter serves the same function as the brochure—it puts you and your program in front of each member of the electorate and asks for his vote. But whereas the brochure is comprehensive and the same one is mailed or handed out to everyone, the direct mail letter can be made more specific and personal.

In preparation for a direct mail campaign, you must obtain all of the lists of names you think necessary to reach. Don't just settle for a list of registered voters or members of your party. You will want to send your letter to them, of course, but there are many others to whom you will want to direct your appeal.

Sandra Hoeh used direct mail effectively in her Milwaukee campaign for city council. She sent out special letters to Jewish and other ethnic groups (her campaign is described in more detail in chapter 20). In your community, you may send special vote-soliciting letters to members of various trade and professional groups. You should send letters to all of the women's organizations in your district, as well as to housewives. You may compile a list of veterans by getting names from local chapters of the American Legion, Veterans of Foreign Wars, Disabled American Veterans, Amvets, World War I Veterans, etc. If your campaign is concerned with home taxation, you will need a special list of home owners. In a school board campaign, lists of property owners, teachers, and parent-teacher association members would be especially useful. In fact, in most community campaigns, all kinds of lists will be helpful to supplement the mailings made to registered voters or members of your political party.

Each group receives a slightly different letter. The salutation and the lead (the first one or two sentences) will vary in order to appeal specifically and personally to that group. If you are a Democrat, you would address your appeal to those of your party as "Dear Fellow Democrat." If you are a veteran, you would address veterans as "Dear Fellow Veteran." Some of your letters can be addressed to "Dear Neighbor" or "Dear Friend."

One way to reduce costs of a direct mail campaign is to use volunteer help in addressing envelopes and for typing in the salutation and opening lines of the letters.

But the important thing to remember in making your direct mail solicitation effective is this: it should be *personal, friendly,* and *persuasive.*

POSTERS, WINDOW CARDS, AND BILLBOARDS

In the average campaign for city, county, and other lower level offices, posters and window cards are much more effective than billboards, and they are also much less expensive. Bumper stickers, once considered an absolute necessity in all kinds of campaigns, are declining in popularity, since car owners do not wish to risk acts of vandalism by persons who do not agree with them politically. This is an unfortunate situation, but it does exist in certain metropolitan areas. Despite the risk of vandalism, yard signs are proving their effectiveness in many urban communities.

One rule holds good for all signs, from the smallest poster to the largest billboard: keep it simple. Because a billboard or road sign is mainly viewed by passing motorists who give it only a quick glance, its message must be an instant one. About all it can project to the passing voter is a picture of the candidate, his or her name, and a four-word slogan or suggestion, such as "Vote for Jane Smith."

Billboards

Any elaborate argument or wordy message on a billboard is a waste of money that could be spent more efficiently in some other form of advertising. But if you feel you must have billboards to sell your face, name, and slogan to the voters, you will have to get an advertising agency to handle the contracts for you in most cases because a number of business considerations are usually involved.

Billboards are most effective in stimulating name identification. So if you are a virtual unknown running against a candidate with wide name recognition, they are considered essential in high-level campaigns. But if you are a candidate for a low-level office in a small town or rural community, other methods will give you more votes for less money.

For example, Ray Gonzales, the Cal State political science teacher, used personalized door-to-door campaigning and other tactics without billboards to defeat the incumbent assemblyman, Kent Stacey. Gonzales spent only $21,000 to Stacey's $100,000. Instead of spending money on big billboards, Gonzales produced a half-hour semi-documentary film on a land conservation problem then worrying Kern County residents, and printed and distributed a four-page tabloid, highlighting the campaign issues and Stacey's legislative record.

Stacey had four times as much money as Gonzales for all types of advertising, but Gonzales relied heavily upon volunteers. His volunteers distributed 60,000 tabloid campaign papers to everyone in the assembly district in a two-week period. One thousand volunteers participated in Gonzales' behalf.

Posters and Window Cards

Nearly all low-budget campaigns use posters and window cards. If you are a candidate for school board or almost any community office, you should plan to use them. They are a simple, effective, and fairly inexpensive means of getting your name and message to the voters. You might even employ a class of young student artists to draw a number of attractive window signs for you. Many stores and shops will let you put a card in their display windows.

If you or your campaign workers decide to tack signs to public utility poles or vacant store fronts in your area, be sure to obtain the consent of the utility companies or store owners. Otherwise you court trouble with the law that could be embarrassing.

Small cards, designed to hang on door knobs, are especially useful in neighborhood canvassing. Using them, canvassers can leave a brief message when no one answers the doorbell. Their message is simple: "Sorry I failed to see you when I called today. Please vote for Bill Smith for Mayor." A campaign folder may be attached to the card with a paper clip.

THE IDEA FILE

One way to help yourself come up with the kind of brochures, posters, and ads you want is to keep an idea file, a collection of campaign material of all kinds. It includes campaign folders, political ads, cards soliciting volunteer workers, newspaper clippings of campaign announcements, publicity stunts, campaign slogans, and, in fact, anything that might suggest a winning campaign idea.

While an honest candidate will never knowingly plagiarize from another candidate's campaign literature, he or she may imitate certain ideas in typographical make-up. In fact, your idea file will be useful in many ways. Its collection of folders and clippings will serve as a springboard for your own creative imagination, thus aiding you in generating new ideas of your own.

15
Organizing an Effective Speaker's Bureau

Regardless of whether you are a candidate for your city school board or for U.S. senator, an organized, energetic speaker's bureau is an important campaign asset. In many cases, it is essential.

Often, in fact, a well-chosen group of skillful, persuasive speakers can do more for a candidate in selling him and his program to the voters than the candidate can do speaking for himself. President McKinley's shrewd campaign manager, Mark Hanna, was one of the first to demonstrate this in a presidential campaign, when he used a team of carefully selected speakers to defeat the great Democratic orator, William Jennings Bryan.

For a local, low-level campaign, you may need fewer than six speakers, but they should be persons who can talk interestingly and convincingly. No fancy, oratorical ability is required. Plain talk is more effective.

Each speaker must be able to make a short speech, emphasizing three points: (1) that you are qualified and right for the office you are seeking; (2) that your program is sound and the right one for solving certain problems of prime importance; and (3) that the solutions to these problems are necessary and in the best interests of those addressed.

THE SPEAKER'S BUREAU CHAIRPERSON

One of your first steps in organizing a speaker's bureau is to employ or otherwise obtain the services of a qualified woman or man to serve as chairperson. The person chosen for this important position should have both executive ability and some political know-how.

The principal duties of the chairperson are as follows:

1. To assist you in recruiting qualified speakers, both men and women.

2. To check with various community organizations—labor, business, veterans, and others—and set up speaking engagements. Your chairperson should appoint a committee of volunteers to telephone all of the main organizations in your community and request permission to have a speaker address their group for five minutes. He or she should also work with outside organizations in providing microphones and like facilities to make the speaking more effective.

3. To train and coach your speakers. This includes assisting speakers in preparing their speech drafts, reminding speakers to go prepared with literature to be distributed at the meetings, and providing any charts or visual aids that may be necessary.

4. To assign appropriate speakers to meetings (that means assigning a union worker, if possible, to labor meeting; a veteran to veterans' gathering; etc.).

5. To cooperate with your publicity department to see that all speaking engagements are given advance publicity and follow-up reports, if possible. He or she should also see that thank-you letters are sent to organizations following the speaking.

6. To check with news reporters and persons attending meetings to see if speakers are doing a good job.

7. To provide a substitute speaker when you are unable to fill one of your own speaking engagements.

8. To work with the director of the house-to-house canvassers to see that the volunteer workers are well informed and know how to present the campaign message tactfully, but effectively.

RECRUITING SPEAKERS

Your next step after selecting a chairperson is to recruit the best qualified speakers available, trying first for volunteers. But if you cannot obtain speakers of the caliber you need, you may have to employ some with your campaign funds. In most cases, it will be money well spent.

Your speakers should be widely representative, but often you will find your best talent among lawyers, student lawyers, and students of public speaking. You should try to include some community leaders in your bureau, especially articulate persons with pleasing voices and personalities. Try to avoid recruiting dull speakers with unpleasant voices or irritating manners. Remember they are your ambassadors of good will.

Here are some of the organizations your speakers will address in an ordinary campaign: labor organizations, business and trade groups, women's organizations, veterans' organizations, PTA groups, political clubs, improvement associations, chamber of commerce and other civic groups, lucheon clubs (Rotary, Kiwanis, etc.), fraternal and religious groups, student associations, consumer affairs clubs, environmentalists and conservationists, senior citizens.

Occasionally, certain groups—particularly luncheon clubs—will object to permitting a speaker because they have a rule not to allow any political speeches. Yet, despite this rule, one of your speakers may obtain permission to speak by promising not to discuss things of a personal or partisan nature. Instead the speaker can discuss an important national or community problem in a way that will show the need for your program, without specifically mentioning you or your program. Although indirect, such a talk is sometimes helpful in creating a favorable public opinion atmosphere for your campaign.

Care must be taken in assigning the right speaker to the group where he or she will be most compatible. Every speaker must be coached about his audience, his subject, and how to key his campaign talk to the group's interest. Your speaker's kit or manual should aid the speaker in doing that.

THE SPEAKER'S KIT

The purpose of a speaker's manual is simply to supply your speakers with "campaign ammunition" and tips on how to do their jobs most successfully. It sets forth facts about the candidate, his stand on the issues, and the most persuasive way to present those facts. In other words, your manual should contain the following information, written clearly and concisely:

1. A brief biographical sketch of the candidate. Tell your place of birth, education, business or professional experience, family status, and political background, if any. Emphasize how your background or experience qualifies you for the office you are seeking and how it *makes you the right person for the job.*

2. Your stand on all important issues involved in the campaign. Emphasize the key issue on which you are basing your main campaign effort, and point out why the voters should be especially concerned with the key issue. Except in rare instances when speaking before groups that are primarily concerned with other issues, *your key campaign issue should be given major emphasis.* Speakers should not get distracted or involved in controversial issues unrelated to your campaign. An attempt to cover too many issues or give too many details will lessen the impact of the speech.

3. Why your program, designed to help solve the major problem, is right and so important to voters being addressed.

4. The weaknesses in your opponent's record and qualifications. However, any personal attack on your opponent may backfire and create sympathy for him. So be careful.

5. Information on how to deal with hecklers, questions, and criticism.

In a big state or federal campaign, slightly different manuals may be prepared for each group, that is, one for labor, one for business, etc. But in a lower-level campaign, one manual can be used for each group. If you have only six speakers, you might use typewritten copies. In a major campaign, they could be mimeographed or reproduced by making photocopies. These manuals are for "insiders only" and not for general circulation.

MAKE 'EM SIT UP AND LISTEN

In your opening words, you need to surprise, excite, or arouse your audience's curiosity with an intriguing question. A good speaker should also try to say something in a way that will stir his listeners and echo through their minds later.

Here are some customary suggestions for speakers:

1. Keep your speeches short.
2. Get immediate attention.
3. Choose a point and make that point.
4. Keep your speech conversational and friendly.
5. Use plain words and short sentences.
6. Clinch your case with a good closing.

While speakers often feel they need more than fifteen minutes to make a point, few are able to hold an audience's attention longer than that. Studies have disclosed that a speaker either wins or loses the interest of his audience in the first two minutes of his speech.

In sitting down to write a speech for a group meeting, the speaker must ask himself these questions:

1. What is the purpose of this talk?
2. What is the main idea I wish to hammer home?
3. How can I tie this idea to something timely, so that I will get immediate interest?
4. What argument will carry the most weight?
5. What proof can I offer?

A campaign speaker should write his speech as he would normally speak, so that it reads smoothly and naturally. Leave out the fancy, hard-to-pronounce words, and use concrete examples and specific cases to prove points. Use picture-words, provocative phrases, and frequent questions in getting your points across to your listeners.

For instance, if the big issue in your campaign is water pollution, your speaker may open with a question like "Have you ever thought how water pollution is affecting your health and that of your children? Scientists have recently discovered that polluted water is one of the major causes of cancer. Scientific tests have shown that fish taken from the lake (or river) which is our source of water contain a chemical residue that is carcinogenic or cancer-causing. Other tests have revealed that this chemical is being put in the water by waste disposal practices of a local industry. George Brown has pledged himself to work for legislation to stop this practice, if elected to the state senate. For your own health and that of your children, vote for George Brown."

To add punch to a speech of this kind, the speaker should specifically name the cancer-causing chemical that has been found in the fish, and read or quote briefly what health authorities have said on the subject.

In publicizing these campaign speeches, give them attention-arousing captions. A provocative or controversial title will often help to stimulate interest.

DISTRIBUTING SPECIAL LITERATURE

If your campaign is for a high-level office, you should have special literature printed for distribution at the meetings addressed by your speakers. For a labor meeting, you should have campaign folders and leaflets setting forth your policies or stands on labor issues. For a women's organization, you should have literature presenting your stand on issues that particularly interest them. But in all of your literature, you should emphasize your key issue.

16
Your Vote-Getting Foot Soldiers

Few elements in a campaign are more important than a well-organized battalion of doorbell-ringing, house-to-house canvassers. They are usually as essential to any political campaign as infantry is to an army. They are needed in pre-election registration drives, primaries, and general elections.

In rural communities and in small cities where your goal is a municipal or county office, your canvassers are often more influential than the media because they are the workers who make direct, personal contact with the voters. Mobilized to act as your private army, utilizing "Fuller Brush" sales tactics, they present a persuasive appeal to every registered voter to vote for you. They do it with tact in a friendly, neighborly manner. Usually, they are volunteers, working for you because they like you, your program, or are loyal members of your party.

The number of foot soldiers you will need will depend on the population of the area covered and the office sought. More than 7,000 canvassers were used in Senator Barry Goldwater's 1958 campaign in Arizona. They canvassed their respective neighborhoods. Approximately 8,000 men and women performed this service in one of Senator Wallace F. Bennett's campaigns in Utah. The safe rule to follow is to recruit as many door-to-door workers as possible, train them, and send them out with instructions to "talk to every voter you can."

Most successful politicians make it a practice to start their canvassing about a month before an election, since it is advisable to reach the undecided voter before he has made up his mind on candidates and issues. But you should not start your canvass until you have some campaign literature printed and available for distribution. This literature will add enormously to the effectiveness of your canvass.

RECRUITING YOUR CANVASSERS

How do you go about recruiting a large volunteer army? You do it by asking your party's help, by seeking the aid of friends and associates, by appealing to those who believe in your cause, by advertising in press and radio for volunteers, and by making a telephone appeal.

It is a good idea to recruit as many active canvassers as you can before calling upon party officials for assistance. In fact, some candidates prefer to select and train their own, since that will give the candidate more authority in directing their efforts. One businesslike procedure for recruiting is to have your campaign manager send out pledge cards to thousands of influential and politically active citizens, asking their aid. But this method can be slow and also expensive due to mailing costs.

In case a reform or moral issue is involved in your campaign, you should try to get church groups interested. Senator Robert S. Kerr of Oklahoma, a Baptist and Prohibitionist, demonstrated years ago that strong campaign support could be obtained this way. Reform movements of almost any kind generate a supply of enthusiastic workers.

If you are a labor-endorsed candidate, you should have little trouble getting the assistance of labor's political action groups. Most labor unions have their political action committees. They continue to play an important role in campaigns, despite new campaign restrictions. COPE, the AFL-CIO political action group, funnels both manpower and money into campaigns that labor has targeted as important.

Still another possible source of volunteer aid is from students who participate in campaign activities to gain political experience.

In a big state or federal campaign for high office, your campaign manager may hire professional workers to augment the volunteer force. There are experienced political canvassers for hire in every large city, but to employ very many would be extremely expensive. Then, too, paid workers are not always as effective as dedicated volunteers working for a cause or a candidate out of loyalty.

INTERVIEWING AND SUPERVISING VOLUNTEERS

When anyone volunteers to work in your campaign, you or one of your associates should interview the volunteer and try to find out in what capacity he or she can serve best. In addition to house-to-house canvassers, you will need volunteer office help to answer phones, address direct mail literature, etc. But your greatest need in volunteer help will be for canvassers.

Keep duplicate file cards (you will find having two sets very helpful) on each volunteer, recording his or her name, address, phone, occupational background, past political experience if any, and the volunteer's work preference. You must also try to give each volunteer some specific task to perform so that he or she will feel useful. Workers must be made to feel they are accomplishing something or they will lose their enthusiasm.

Of course, you will need a competent supervisor to train, direct, and assign your canvassers to their precinct activities. Often it is advisable to employ a professional who can assist you in organizing and recruiting your canvassers. But in a small town or rural community, this important role of campaigning is sometimes performed very successfully by a popular club woman with executive ability. Experience in conducting Red Cross or parent-teacher club drives is an excellent qualification.

THE REGISTRATION DRIVE

Before sending out your canvassers, you should obtain from your party officials, if possible, up-to-date information regarding the names of persons living in the area to be canvassed, the party affiliation of voters, and names of registered and unregistered voters.

In using this information during your canvass, you will have as one of your objectives the early registration of all members of your party still unregistered. During every interview with a prospective voter, the canvasser should ask, "Have you registered to vote in the coming election?"

If not, he should be urged to do so at once. If the man of the house is a member of your party, a special effort should be made to register all members of the family eligible to vote. If your workers find a high percentage of persons in the area still unregistered, a special drive should be started to get them registered, unless they are members of the opposite party and unlikely to vote for you. Naturally, if you are a Republican running in a district that has two Democrats for every Republican, you will not be helping your candidacy by urging a big registration drive.

Aiding independents to register may be very helpful. To assist voters in getting registered, it is essential that you and your workers know the rules governing registration requirements and procedures in your state. You will need to know residential requirements, places of registration, when registration begins and closes, and "change of address" regulations.

But you must not depend entirely upon your party lists of registered voters. Your workers should knock on every door. Otherwise your canvass will be incomplete and only partially effective.

CANVASSING PROCEDURES

Before being sent into the field, canvassers must be given certain basic information. This includes a brief biography of the candidate, including his or her qualifications for the office sought; a description of the key issues and the candidate's program; and information on how to answer questions concerning issues. Your canvassers should carry campaign literature with them to distribute to voters.

Rules for Canvassing

Here are a few recommended rules for canvassing:

1. Get the name of occupant before knocking on the door, if possible. A next-door neighbor may be your best source of

information, although voters' registration lists, names on mailboxes, or telephone directories may provide this information.

2. Quickly introduce yourself and smile as you explain the purpose of your call. One way to get off to a good start is to ask the voter about some question of vital importance to the community or the nation.

3. Tell him or her briefly about the candidate, the candidate's program, and why it is important to the community or the nation.

4. Find out if the voter is registered. Try to get him registered if he's of your party and for your candidate.

5. Answer voter's questions if you can. If you don't know, say so, and offer to find out and send him an answer.

6. Don't interfere with social or family affairs. Make your call brief—not over five minutes.

7. Try to call on at least ten homes a day.

8. Try to get the voter to express his opinion on issues, but do not argue. Remember the voter has the right to differ.

9. Leave some campaign literature and leave with a smile.

10. Always carry cards or a notebook on which to make a brief record of your visit.

11. Never knock on a stranger's door after 9:30 p.m.

There are practical and psychological reasons for those eleven canvassing rules. Most persons welcome an opportunity to be interviewed and feel flattered and pleased that a candidate should seek their opinion. That is why the canvasser is advised to open the conversation at the door with a question about a local or national concern. It is a good way to get immediate attention.

Continuing in a conversational tone, the canvasser may say something like this: "I find many people in the community are deeply concerned about high food prices, gasoline prices, and unemployment. My candidate, Mr. Brown, is especially concerned about those matters and he is pledged to work for solutions, if elected."

Should the voter insist on an answer to a question and the canvasser doesn't know the answer, the canvasser should say, "I'll try to find out and let you know."

The rule not to interfere in family social or business affairs covers a number of things. For instance, if the family is having a late breakfast or an early evening meal, or if the baby is being bathed, the canvasser might say: "I beg your pardon for coming to see you at this time. I'm distributing literature for Mr. Brown, candidate for ————, and will call back later." The canvasser leaves some literature and leaves with a smile.

That rule to smile when introducing yourself and again in leaving is based on sound, time-tested psychology. Persons with friendly smiles and outgoing personalities are much more successful in house-to-house canvassing. The smiling approach works wonders.

What Hours Are Best?

Early evening hours are generally considered best, but in deciding which hours are best for your campaign, you must take into consideration the living habits in your community where the canvass is to be made. Several factors determine which hours are best for calls.

In a dairying area, your canvassers would have to exercise care not to call when the family would be busy with milking chores. And if the neighborhood is one in which there are many nightworkers who sleep during daylight hours, that, too, must be taken into consideration. *One of the cardinal rules of successful canvassing is not to annoy people.*

If your foot soldiers are concentrating on women's votes, they should make day calls when the men are away at work. But if they feel reaching male voters is more important, they may have to make their house calls between 7 p.m. and 9 p.m., although those hours present problems, too. Some men who commute to and from work have just arrived home from work. They may be taking a shower, eating dinner, or watching a favorite show or news broadcast, and don't wish to be interrupted.

Women canvassers should not be sent alone into certain neighborhoods at night, and in some areas your workers should canvass in pairs. Insurance agents and Jehovah Witnesses frequently canvass in this manner. The method to be used in your canvass will be dictated to some extent by the nature of the area and its violent crime rate.

State Representative Edward M. Early, who personally knocked on nearly every door in his district, a Pittsburgh suburb, during his campaigns, believes he accomplished his most effective canvassing on weekends. He said his average stay at a home varied from a few seconds to fifteen minutes. His formula was to introduce himself quickly, explain why he was a candidate and say, "I would appreciate it if you would consider voting for me."

He believes it is better to ask the voter to "consider" voting for him, instead of flatly asking the voter to vote for him. He always made it a point to state his party affiliation. While this is important in a primary, it might be harmful in a general election when your party is the minority one in registration. In that case, it would be better not to emphasize your party identification unless you are certain the voter being interviewed is a member of your party.

How Should They Dress?

Canvassers should dress neatly. Clean casual or working clothes are considered the appropriate attire for canvassers in a low-income residential area, while for an upper-income district, a coat and tie may be better for male canvassers. The main idea is to dress neatly and in keeping with the style of the neighborhood, so that the canvasser will seem to belong to the community and not be an outsider.

For the same reason, that of belonging, an elderly doorbell ringer will get a better reception in a community of elderly citizens, especially during evening hours when many older persons are afraid to let strangers into their homes. Some housewives are likewise cautious about inviting anyone in, or even unlatching a screen door to accept a piece of campaign literature. Many big city candidates have become equally cautious and instruct their male canvassers never to go into a home where a young lady is alone. They fear "political entrapment."

Maintaining Records

Your canvassers should record on a card or in a notebook the correct names of those visited, date and time of call, and whether they seemed favorable to your candidacy. It should also report whether or not the voter is registered.

Most big city political bosses have expected their canvassers to gather much more information than this. They wanted their precinct workers to find out the number of members in a family and even their birthdays, so that a ward official of the machine could drop around later and offer birthday congratulations. This was all a part of the boss's "buttering-up" formula for reaching the heart-strings of his constituents. Workers were also expected to find out if the family needed welfare assistance. The boss would try to provide that help. That was one way he maintained power.

Your canvassers can also help you by jotting down information in their notebooks about the needs of the voters in your area and their opinions on key issues.

The canvasser, however, must be advised to be careful about making any notes in the presence of the person being interviewed, unless it is explained that the note is taken so that the candidate can be reminded of some suggestion made by the voter. Care must be taken because some persons are suspicious of anyone taking notes. Cards are often preferred over notebooks for note taking because the information can be more conveniently filed.

CANVASSING BY TELEPHONE

In case you find it impossible to conduct a house-to-house canvass because you cannot recruit enough workers or you are unable to get permission to make house calls in certain apartment buildings and condominiums, then you can have your workers make a canvass by telephone. While the results are never as good as those obtained by personal contact, they can be made highly productive if you will supplement the phone calls with printed literature mailed to those called. The phone calls should be made by persons selected and trained for this job. Both men and women have demonstrated that they can do this phase of campaigning successfully.

In making these calls, the campaign worker quickly identifies himself or herself and may begin by asking the voter's opinion about a problem or current issue. The caller may also ask how the voter regards the candidates and tactfully put in a good word for his candidate. If the voter declares himself in favor of your opponent, the canvasser offers no argument. Instead he may say, "I trust Mr. Brown. I think he is honest and capable, and I intend to vote for him."

The important thing that the caller must do is to make a single, positive statement in behalf of the candidate he is working for, and leave the voter in a friendly mood. Phone calls, like house visits, should be brief. The caller ends the conversation by thanking the voter for his or her opinion.

A standard, routine type of sales or campaign spiel is never as effective as a natural, more informal approach.

Phone drives can also be used at other stages of your campaign. They are especially needed to get every member of your party registered to vote; to remind all of your supporters to be sure to vote on election day; to help raise finances; and to boost attendance at public meetings, pep meetings, parades and rallies.

Training Your Phone Crew

Since you may have to depend principally upon volunteers for your telephone solicitors, you cannot always be too selective, so you will have to make the best of what you have. That means you must select those available who seem most promising and train them to do the job.

It is most important that the members of your phone crew sound friendly and natural. You can help make the job easy and fool-proof by giving them a short, typewritten script of what they are expected to say when making their calls. *But this is not to be read over the phone.* Rather it is to be presented in a conversational tone and manner. To be effective, it must sound natural, not affected or recited by rote.

The natural effect is aided by pausing after each sentence for just a moment to let the idea sink in. To keep from sounding monotonous, the tone should vary slightly in pitch. Of course, a special effort should be made to speak clearly.

The goal of the house-to-house canvass and the phone campaign is achieved when you've reached every voter in your area with your message.

17
Should You Debate Your Opponent?

"Shall I debate my opponent?" Nearly every candidate for public office is confronted with that question sometime during the campaign.

If you are running against a well-known incumbent, you may hope to gain favorable publicity and wider voter recognition by debating him. On the other hand, if you are the better-known office holder and are facing an aggressive campaigner, you may hesitate to challenge or accept a challenge to debate. Debating is a very risky business. Consequently, the attitude of the incumbent toward debating is usually negative. "I can't afford to let that unknown get publicity by debating me," the incumbent may explain to friends. "That would be stupid. I'm well known to the voters and he's not. It would be all gain for him."

But this typical attitude—that a debate nearly always favors the challenger—is not always true. In many cases it may be, but the question of who will benefit depends upon several factors— namely, which one is the best debater; which one has the best case or the most popular side of the basic issues; which one has the most charisma or the more attractive personality; which one is the most vulnerable or has some weak spot in his background that may be exposed in a public debate; and which one makes the best preparation for the debate.

These are some of the things you must consider before you

challenge or accept a challenge to debate your opponent. You must carefully weigh all of these factors in reaching a decision.

If you are confident of your ability as a debater and believe you have the popular side of the key issues, you should challenge your opponent to a debate, especially if he is an incumbent. The debate will provide you with a forum for putting him and his record on trial before the voters. Remember Richard Nixon, Shirley Chisholm, Abraham Lincoln, and many others made their entries into politics by their debating skills.

Instead of challenging your opponent to debate you on television or radio, you may find a public hall in your community for the debate. One sponsored by the League of Women Voters or some other nonpartisan organization will help assure an audience.

Remember, though, that in a television debate, you are going to be on your own, without the aid of prompters—human or electronic. And since television debating is both expensive and risky, you will be wise in a campaign for a low-level office to put most of your campaign money into house-to-house canvassing, radio or newspaper publicity and advertising, direct mail, and telephone solicitation.

However, the debate may be the very thing you need to demonstrate that you are the right man or woman for the job you seek. But risks are involved, and the debate route is not for everyone.

THE BLUFFING GAME

In case you feel certain your opponent will not accept a challenge to debate the issues, you may challenge him anyway, then capitalize on his rejection of your challenge in your publicity. That will put him in a defensive position, giving voters the impression that he has something to hide or lacks confidence in his stand on the issues. Often, however, an incumbent who is reluctant to debate is prodded into accepting the debate challenge because he fears this form of voter reaction.

On the other hand, *you* may be the one challenged. If you are not sure of your debating skill, or have some doubt about your ability to defend your record or program in a public debate, then you must counter your opponent's efforts to draw you into a debate as a "cheap publicity gimmick to revive interest in his sagging campaign." To divert attention from his debate challenge, you must use newspaper, radio, and every other form of advertising and publicity open to you to challenge him and his program, and to sell your own.

DEBATING TIPS

If, after careful consideration of your campaign situation, you decide that a debate with your adversary is necessary in order to win, you must adequately prepare and practice for it.

The major essentials for successful debating are a complete and accurate knowledge of the subject to be discussed; a definite, carefully thought-out plan of presentation; skill in expressing your viewpoint in a convincing manner; anticipation of your opponent's arguments and questions; and good physical condition (take a nap in the afternoon before your night debate, and remember that your audience will probably be impressed as much by how you look as by what you say).

In sum, you must be sure of yourself, know your facts, and be well prepared.

Here are some tips for debating your opponent. Use them in planning and preparing your presentation.

1. Attack your opponent's record. Put him on the defensive.

2. Once you've seized the offensive, continue to press the attack relentlessly.

3. Anticipate questions and have your answers ready.

4. Rehearse with a good debater before the debate.

5. Look toward your audience and speak to them instead of to your opponent during the debate.

CHOOSING THE RIGHT DEBATE FORMAT

Since debates come in different forms—traditional or modernized—try to use the debate format that seems best for you. The traditional pattern permits opponents to draw straws or otherwise decide who will make the opening statement, which runs from eight to ten minutes, followed by a brief rebuttal. If you are better with prepared, partially memorized speeches, this form will probably be better for you than a debate requiring ad lib responses to questions by persons chosen as interrogators. Many of the so-called political debates now in vogue are much more like press conferences or "meet-the-press" programs than a debate. In these programs, a panel of interrogators puts questions to the candidates. Another modern form of "debate" is to employ the panel questioning pattern, with each candidate being allowed to make a final statement, summing up their points.

After the form of the debate has been outlined, you should begin formulating your speech to comply with the time limits. It must emphasize your program clearly and persuasively.

When it comes your time to speak during the debate, be prepared to *start talking immediately.* Don't try to make too many points. Concentrate on the important, basic issues—the ones that will win you votes, those in which your listeners are most interested. If you try to make too many points, you will scatter your fire.

EXPOSING YOUR OPPONENT'S WEAK POINTS

A good example of how a candidate can use a debate to expose his opponent's record occurred in California in 1976. During the Democratic primary, Senator John Tunney found himself being strongly challenged by Tom Hayden, an anti-war activist and former defendant in "The Chicago Seven" trial following the riots at the Democratic National Convention in 1968. Investigation convinced Tunney that many conservatives in the party were supporting Hayden because they did not remember his activist background. So the senator, who had been rejecting Hayden's challenges to debate, decided to debate Hayden in the hope of using the television forum to expose Hayden's seemingly forgotten record.

Three television reporters participated in the confrontation that took place on KNBC, June 5, 1976. In the debate, Tunney was successful in spotlighting Hayden's activist background. Marvin D. Field, director of the California Poll, later credited the TV debate as being a decisive factor in Tunney's primary victory over Hayden. It can be cited as one instance in which an incumbent gained votes through a television debate. Later, in the 1976 general election, Tunney debated his Republican opponent, Dr. Hayakawa, but lost.

LEARN BY WATCHING

One excellent way to improve your own debating techniques is to watch political debates on television and listen to those on radio. You may have been one of the millions who watched the Carter-Ford presidential debates on television in 1976. When they ended, the consensus of opinion, according to surveys and newspaper reports, was that Carter had won. Carter aids claimed that the final debate was a clear-cut victory for Carter. Ford representatives said it was a tie. It was generally conceded, however, that Ford made one serious blunder in the final debate when he said that Europe's communist bloc nations were not Soviet-dominated. This statement, made in the heat of the debate, alienated many immigrants from those nations, costing Ford probably a million votes.

Consequently, one lesson to be learned from the Carter-Ford debates is that a single mis-statement of fact in a debate can be crucial. Remember, you must be certain of your facts.

Nixon lost his famous first debate with John F. Kennedy in Chicago on September 26, 1960 for far different reasons. Perhaps the basic reason he lost to Kennedy was that he could not match Kennedy's charisma. But in the first four of the televised debates, Nixon was recovering from an illness and was poorly prepared for a television appearance. He was several pounds below his regular weight, his shirt collar sagged, and the studio lights seemed to exaggerate the dark circles under his eyes. And although he had just shaved, his TV make-up failed to conceal the roots of his beard under his pallid complexion. This gave him an unshaven appearance. Moreover, Nixon seemed nervous in contrast to Kennedy's calm, self-confident behavior.

Nixon added to his problems by appearing to address his remarks to his adversary rather than to his television audience. Kennedy, by contrast, looked straight at the audience, so television viewers felt they were being directly addressed. This is another lesson to remember: look at your audience, not at your opponent.

Another rule to remember in television debating, or any debating for that matter, is to *keep calm and behave naturally*. Try not to let your opponent ruffle you or make you lose your temper. Both Carter and Ronald Reagan projected calm, self-confident personalities in 1976, speaking softly and smiling frequently. In fact, they seemed to project a bland, almost imperturbable attitude during questioning by news persons, even when some of the questions seemed deliberately worded to ruffle them.

Commenting upon this trait that both Carter and Reagan shared, Thomas Griffin, author of "Newswatch" in *Time,* June 28, 1976, wrote: "In part because of their professional, almost impersonal skill at merchandising their personalities, they create an aura of reserve about themselves—one that reporters rarely penetrate. Against their cool responses, interrogative reporting of the Mike Wallace–Dan Rather school seems out of season, overheated and hectoring. Reporters, themselves often on camera, vie with the candidates in not wishing to appear rash, partisan or unfair."

Certainly in a debate, whether on television or on a public speaking platform, a candidate must be careful not to appear rash, unduly partisan, or unfair. The TV camera seems to magnify anything of an unnatural or discordant nature.

18
Generating Enthusiasm for Victory

Like a pep rally before a football game, political rallies, parades, and demonstrations serve a very useful purpose in stimulating the last-minute enthusiasm and fervor necessary to get your supporters to the polls. The enthusiasm they generate also radiates out, converting some of the luke-warm or apathetic voters, as well as nonpartisan independents.

Their usefulness is not confined just to getting voters to the polls on election day. They enliven the kick-off, the initiation of the campaign, and inspire workers to greater effort during registration drives and other crucial stages in the battle for votes.

PLANNING AN EFFECTIVE RALLY

A rally or a demonstration of any kind has to be well organized and publicized, and the timing must be right, if the rally is to accomplish its purpose.

Timing
Timing of the rally is of major importance, especially in the closing period of the campaign. Many campaigns have been lost by faulty timing. For if enthusiasm is generated to a high point too early in a campaign and peaks prematurely, the fervor needed for the final push to get the voters to the polls on election day may

have evaporated. Lacking enthusiasm, there is a psychological letdown. Such a sag in enthusiasm on the day of decision can be fatal to a candidate.

Recent studies of the decision-making processes of voters have indicated that about 17 percent of the total vote does not jell until the last five days of the campaign. Up to that time, this percentage of the electorate is still undecided. That is the period when rallies, parades, and demonstrations are the most decisive. It is instinctive for many voters to want to get on the band wagon or the victory train. They like to identify with the winners. At the rallies in the closing days of a campaign, speakers and placards can emphasize the slogan "Join the winning team."

Preparing for the Rally

Of course, any kind of a mass meeting or demonstration demands careful planning and an energetic, promotional buildup through every available means. The more punch you can put into the preparation and promotion, the more successful the event will be.

The proper preparation for a rally requires:

1. Selection of a good central location, easily accessible and with adequate parking accommodations. The hall, auditorium, or outside area chosen should be sufficiently large to accommodate a gathering of the size expected. Too small a hall will be impractical, and one that is much too large for you to fill may leave the impression that you and your cause are unpopular. So you must consider these factors in choosing your meeting place.

2. Selection of a well-equipped location. Be sure that the place is equipped with all of the necessary speaking facilities—a platform, microphone with electronic amplifier, chairs, table, and lighting.

3. A supply of banners, placards, and campaign literature carrying your name and campaign slogan, and small balloons if you can afford them.

4. A group of well-trained cheer leaders, who will be coached before the rally on how to lead the applause and excite enthusiastic demonstrations.

5. One or more animated speakers. This is one of the prime requirements for any successful political rally. If possible, the candidate should make a brief, inspiring speech as the feature of the rally. His or her speech should be the keynote of the affair. It might follow a few brief speeches by others. For a big rally, you could follow the format of a national party convention.

Make Sure You're the Star

In an earlier chapter, it was mentioned that Wilbert Lee O'Daniel used hillbilly bands and well-organized "sings" to animate his campaigns in Texas, which were very successful. But he always followed up with a rousing, hard-hitting speech that promised his hearers a better life.

This raises a point that needs emphasis. A candidate must not put on such a big show that it eclipses him or what he has to say. The candidate and his speech outlining his program should be the highlight of the occasion.

Your rally must be more than a show—after all, its purpose is to win votes. A gigantic rally has little political significance unless the candidate staging it can use the rally to publicize himself and promote a program attractive to voters. In 1974, Herbert Hafif, a Claremont, California attorney who had attracted wide attention by winning large damage suits for his clients, decided to seek the Democratic nomination for governor. To announce his candidacy, he planned a mammoth pop concert-rally to be held in Long Beach. Hiring some of the country's top rock singers, he spent several thousand dollars on full-page daily newspaper ads, along with radio and television publicity, promoting the rally. It was to be the biggest political rally of its kind on record.

On the night of his extraordinary musical-political extravaganza, a large crowd—estimated by some to be in excess of 30,000—gathered at the Long Beach setting. Many of those coming from various parts of the state were youthful music lovers. From a promotional and pop music viewpoint, the event was a great success. From a political view, it was a flop.

Hafif had put on a good show, but he had failed to formulate an attractive, convincing, vote-getting campaign program. He was eclipsed by his own show and was soon only an "also ran." He did receive good publicity, though, and since lawyers at the time were not permitted to advertise, this was no doubt beneficial.

The lesson is clear. Your rallies, demonstrations, and parades must spotlight you and your program, and your program has to be designed to get votes. If you have induced a prominent entertainer to participate in your rally in order to draw a crowd, make certain that your program is so arranged that you, the candidate, are not eclipsed by the celebrity.

Parade Permits

In many areas, parade permits are not required, but if they are, get them well in advance of the event. Try to make your parades unusual, attention-getting events, employing a high school band when possible to add to the festive air. Colorful costumes will help enliven the parade.

Using Floats and Banners

In your parades and demonstrations, you can call attention to your program or key campaign issue not only with banners and placards but also with floats. For instance, you can focus attention on inflation with a Mother Goose float. The lady dressed as Mother Goose stands on the float near an enormous shoe, cut from cardboard. Heads of children appear at windows of the cardboard shoe house. Signs call attention to the problem of inflation and how it is hurting everyone. Mother Goose has a staff carrying a banner reading: "Vote against inflation! Vote for John Jones—He is pledged to work for *Economy in Government.*" A Mother Goose float could also be used in calling attention to the housing shortage that now plagues many communities.

All kinds of ideas can be expressed by floats. Like billboards, they should make their point and convey their message in as few words as possible.

If you are a candidate for Congress, you may wish to campaign on the issue of reducing government bureaucracy. This idea can be illustrated by having a girl on a float cutting a red ribbon with a large pair of scissors. A banner on the float would explain: "Let's Cut the Bureaucratic Red Tape. Elect John Jones."

Or you can dramatize the idea of the need for jobs. On the float are two doors. One with a placard reading "No Jobs" is closed.

The other, with a few persons in rags waiting in front of it, is marked "Food Stamps." The main banner on the float truck reads: "Give Us Jobs, Not Food Stamps."

In a campaign for mayor or city council, you may wish to call attention to crime, police department graft, inadequate fire protection, high property taxes, governmental inefficiency, or any number of things that can be represented on floats. Inadequate fire protection could be portrayed by a large picture showing a house in flames while lying nearby on the ground is a fire hose with only a trickle of water coming from the nozzle.

Spread the Word

Once you have all of the preparations under way for making your rally, demonstration, or parade a success, publicize the event thoroughly—by newspaper and radio publicity, handbills, telephone calls, direct mail, and, in some cases, by paid advertising and sound trucks. Try to enlist extensive participation by various community organizations.

ORGANIZING A SPECIAL CARAVAN

One variation of the rally is the traveling caravan—a number of automobiles and buses carrying your supporters to various public places. Accompanied, perhaps, by a school band and equipped with banners, it carries your campaign to a neighboring community. You might make the event even more exciting by having a torchlight parade precede the speaking at the rally.

Caravan rallies of this kind have been used successfully in fund-collecting drives as well as in generating enthusiasm for the closing days of the campaign. Always try to get a band of some kind for these neighborhood rallies. Band music gives a festive air to the event and helps attract a friendly, receptive crowd.

Planning the Program

When your caravan arrives at the site chosen for the speaking and a crowd gathers, the person chosen to serve as special program chairman mounts the platform and calls for order. Usually you will be greeted by a committee, and their spokesman, an official of the community, will make a brief speech of welcome. He or she will introduce you or the person speaking in your behalf. The introductory speech should be brief.

You or your representative then makes a 15-minute speech, emphasizing a major concern of the citizens of the community, and your promise to help solve the problem, if elected. You may also denounce the failure of your opponent to do anything about it, if he is an incumbent. In case he is not an incumbent, you may point out the weakness in his proposed solution to the problem that is causing voter concern. Close with a call for action, whether you are asking for campaign funds, urging them to register, or to vote. Your speech should be designed to boost morale and win additional support. Speak with confidence and enthusiasm.

Maintaining the Schedule

In a caravan tour that makes several stops at shopping centers, courthouses, and industrial plants, try to maintain your publicized schedule and not be late. Enthusiasm rapidly evaporates when your caravan is an hour late in arriving.

If some unforeseen incident slows your caravan down and you see you cannot reach a scheduled speech-stop on time, telephone a friend or supporter and have him make an announcement. Try to encourage those who have assembled to wait a little longer.

By using a sound truck or a van equipped with a loud speaker, you can cover a fairly large area in a day. But sound trucks require a special permit in many communities, and they have become so common that they stir little interest. The caravan is a much more effective device for encouraging campaign activity and arousing enthusiasm.

OTHER MORALE-BUILDING EVENTS

Throughout your campaign, and especially in the closing days, coffee hours, cocktail parties, and special dinners are useful in building morale and inspiring teamwork. Yet in some communities, particularly in Amish and Mormon settlements or when working with strong church support, the cocktail party is definitely not the thing.

Another variation of the customary rally is to hold a number of smaller rallies for special groups—one for labor, another for professional people, a third for farmers, etc. Special rallies for women, young people, or senior citizens may be arranged. For the labor rally, you should have as your speaker a labor leader who is supporting your candidacy.

A FIGHTING FINISH

Enthusiasm is one of the keys to success in any kind of campaign activity, and it is particularly needed in the closing days to stir the voters and get them to the polls. Rallies, demonstrations, and parades are the favorite techniques for doing that.

Yet care must be taken not to create overconfidence among your workers, causing them to let down because they think victory is within easy reach. It is usually safer to "run scared" and to exhort your workers to close the gap by redoubling their efforts. The task requires delicate psychological balancing. Some campaign workers get discouraged and tend to give up when they begin to think their efforts are futile. In your pep talks to them, you must emphasize that a fighting finish is required to win.

19
Vote Fraud

Since you never win an election until all of the votes are counted, you must take the necessary precautionary steps to make sure that the ballots that are counted have been cast by legitimate, qualified voters. That means that you and your poll watchers must know the election laws of your state and county and be on guard against all of the customary tricks of those who make a practice of stealing elections.

There was a time, not too distant, when big-city and rural-area political bosses stole elections by stuffing ballot boxes, casting votes in the names of dead persons copied from gravestones, or brazenly buying the votes of booze-thirsty derelicts. Although many of these bosses have died or passed from power, the practice of vote stealing is not completely dead. It still occurs, but less frequently.

Remember the example of Jimmy Carter, who went to court to overturn a suspected rigged election in Georgia when he made his first bid for election to the state senate in 1962. *Time* magazine reported on May 31, 1971, that "Carter had been beaten by voters who were dead, jailed, or never at the polls on Election Day. The election was reversed." If Carter had permitted the first count in that Georgia election to have gone unchallenged, he very likely would never have become president of the United States, for his start in politics would have been blunted and discouraged.

You, too, could find your career in politics thwarted, perhaps ruined, if you allow your first election to be stolen.

HOW TO PREPARE FOR A POLL WATCH

Unless you have strong party backing and your county party organization has a competent team of well-trained poll watchers assigned to maintain a vigilant check on all of the polling places in your district, you may have to organize and train your own. Even if your county organization is supposed to be taking care of this responsibility, you should check just how thoroughly it is being done.

If you find that you are going to have to organize and train your own, you should have it completed at least three days before election day. Other preparations for the poll watch should also be completed by that time. To prepare for your poll watch:

1. Get a copy of the specific laws governing watching in your district, and make certain that the people you select to perform this duty know the laws so that they will know how to conduct themselves properly and know how to proceed in challenging voters who arouse their suspicion. They also need to know how to respond if challenged by election board officials.

2. Provide each poll watcher with a list of all qualified voters in the district, including a list of those recently registered.

3. Give each watcher your telephone number or that of the party's election district captain in charge of voting in the precinct, and also the phone number of campaign headquarters.

4. Instruct each watcher as to specific kinds of illegal voting to be especially on guard against, and how to detect cheaters. This instruction should be given in a special training class by a person who is familiar with local voting practices.

5. Assign two poll watchers, with alternates or substitutes, to each polling place, and make certain they are given proper credentials authorizing them to act as your or the party's official representatives.

6. Make certain that your poll watchers arrive at their assigned places a half hour before the polls open for voting and that they remain there during their assigned time, or until the

final tally of votes is completed. Each poll watcher should understand his or her duties for each hour the polls are open on election day, and they must never leave the polling place without a substitute on duty.

In most communities, a board of commissioners or an election official is in charge of elections. They may operate under their own legal authority or under the general supervision of a county or city clerk. The official in charge supervises the way the election is conducted. Usually, the polling place officials are election júdges, inspectors, clerks serving in various capacities, watchers, and challengers.

The voting procedures are supervised by the judges, inspectors, and clerk, who have been officially appointed and given some training for their duties.

The watchers and challengers may be the legal representatives of political parties, the candidates, and civic organizations, such as the League of Women Voters. A limited number of party representatives in addition to watchers may be permitted inside the voting place. But to have the right to sit inside the polling place observing what is taking place, making notes, and challenging, the watchers and challengers must have proper credentials. This tends to give an advantage to candidates who are party members over the independent candidate.

Unfortunately, many citizens, and sometimes even those officially appointed to handle the voting, know little about election rules. Consequently, careless and untrained persons appointed to serve on the election staff may commit errors that may invalidate an election. Also, their ignorance of proper procedure may permit a crooked politician to steal an election. Bosses have been known to maneuver to get their stooges and confederates appointed to act as judge or inspector, thus facilitating the vote theft.

THE POLL WATCHER'S PROCEDURE

The poll watcher arrives at the polling place thirty minutes before the polls open. He or she has a complete list of all voters registered in the precinct. He has paper and pencil, and coins for phone calls that may be necessary. He presents his credentials to the inspector and to the police officer on duty. He makes a note of the names of election officers on duty, jotting down the badge number of the policeman. He then checks the ballot box to see that it is empty, and notes that the counters on the voting machines register zero. Before the voting starts, he takes a seat near the judges' table. As each voter signs the register to get his ballot, one of the judges calls out the name and address. The watcher checks it against his precinct list. If the name of the would-be voter is not on his precinct list, he challenges it *in a courteous, businesslike manner*. If the election officials disregard his challenge, he reports what is taking place to you or to his precinct captain.

TYPES OF VOTE FRAUD

Although most election officials are fair, a candidate's watchers must always be alert for tricks. The most common methods of cheating are stuffing the ballot box or tampering with the voting machine so that it registers false votes; giving improper instructions or "assistance" to voters seeking aid; buying votes; falsely counting and recording election results; and denying legitimate voters the right to vote, while permitting unqualified voters to do so.

The "Assistance" Tactic

The "assistance" tactic is used by election-stealers in the following manner. Persons who have agreed to sell their vote are sent to the polls with specific instructions to ask for assistance, offering various excuses. The "assistance" is then provided by an election official who is a confederate of the vote-theft boss. The official sees that the vote is for the boss's favored candidate. The watcher must make sure that the request for assistance is justified by some legitimate reason. If it seems unjustified, the voter can be challenged to sign an affidavit certifying that some impairment makes help necessary.

Forged Vote Applications

A corrupt election official may permit a vote-stealer to take applications for ballots the night before an election. The names of voters are then forged as signatures on the applications. Using these applications, the vote-stealer then obtains a corresponding number of ballots and votes them. This method of vote-stealing can only be accomplished with the connivance of corrupt election officials.

Forged vote applications are also used by "repeaters and stingers," as they are called. This trick is to vote several times in one day by using a forged application. Repeaters can be caught by an alert poll watcher.

Illegal Vote Solicitation

Vote solicitation within less than 100 feet of the entrance to a polling place is illegal in many communities. This bars use of signs, leaflets, loud speakers on trucks, and all forms of solicitation.

Ballot Counting Fraud

Many of the big vote-steals occur after the closing of the polls. What happens sometimes resembles sleight-of-hand. The boxes holding the ballots may be switched, removed, and altered during an evening lunch hour, prior to the counting. Or crooked, conniving election judges may call a vote count incorrectly as they report the vote to the clerks tallying the count. Cheating clerks may also tally the votes falsely. The poll watcher must be alert for all kind of tricks.

In case there is suspicion that a vote-steal is being attempted, a watcher should accompany the election officials who take the votes and records to the board of election commissioners. This is to make sure that no alterations are made en route.

False Statements of Residence

Although it is a criminal offense to make a false statement of residence in order to qualify as a voter, cheaters often do just that. A post-election investigation revealed that more than 500 persons voted in one North Dakota city in 1960 on affidavits of residence that appeared to be false. Investigators were unable to find them at those addresses, and some of the addresses were nonexistent.

Investigations of other elections have revealed that persons recorded as voting had been dead for years.

THE CASE OF BOX 13

One case of alleged vote stealing that got national attention in 1948 and for sometime thereafter occurred in Jim Wells County, Texas. There, votes in box 13 became crucial in a near tie vote between Lyndon B. Johnson and former Texas governor Coke R. Stevenson in an August runoff primary contest for U.S. Senator. In the June Democratic primary, Stevenson and Johnson had emerged the high candidates, with Stevenson far in the lead. But in the August runoff, an unofficial report compiled by the Texas Election Bureau showed Stevenson leading Johnson by 113 votes. Johnson, however, claimed victory, and a recount of the Jim Wells County vote in box 13 added 202 votes to Johnson's total. That put the final tally of votes at 494,191 for Johnson to 494,104 for Stevenson.

Stevenson and his supporters immediately challenged this recount, and two ex-FBI men and a Texas Ranger were sent to Jim Wells County to investigate. The ballots and election records were under armed guard in the bank of George Parr, of Alice, Texas. Parr, known as the political boss of Jim Wells and Duval counties, refused the investigators access to the records. When the investigators later gained access to them by court order, they allegedly found that while the recount vote showed 967 votes for Johnson, only 600 persons had been registered to vote in the 13th precinct. They also found that some of those listed as voting had died prior to the election.

A long court hassle over the alleged vote fraud then began in Texas, but certain Jim Wells election officials had gone to Mexico, presumably on business. U.S. Supreme Court Justice Hugo L. Black finally resolved the controversy in favor of Johnson by staying a lower court order for a thorough investigation. Abe Fortas, who acted as Johnson's attorney in appealing to Justice Black, was subsequently appointed to the Supreme Court by Johnson when he became president. Meanwhile, the questionable voting records of precinct 13 had been burned "by accident." George Parr committed suicide in 1975, when his fraudulent practices were exposed.

Verification of this vote fraud appeared in a July 31, 1977, Associated Press article. It reported that Luis Salas, former election judge in precinct 13, admitted to the AP that he had certified enough fictitious ballots to steal the election for Johnson. It was this election that launched Johnson on this path to the presidency.

Previous articles have covered the case in detail—namely, Clyde Wantland's "The Story of George Parr's Ballot Box No. 13" (*Texas Argus,* April 1962), and George Schendel's "Something Rotten in the State of Texas" (*Collier's,* June 9, 1951). In his book, *A Texan Looks at Lyndon,* J. Evetts Haley credits this incident with changing history.

Fortunately, elections appear to be getting cleaner. But the lesson in past incidents of vote-stealing is *don't leave anything to chance or to crooked politics in the polling place. Be on guard against carelessness and fraud.*

20
The Local Campaign—A Review

In every kind of a campaign—whether for a city council seat or for president—the main purpose is identical. The candidate is trying to convince the voters that his or her program is the best one for them. Both local and national campaigns are organized efforts in personal salesmanship, aimed at selling an image and a program.

But there are a few major differences between local and national campaigns:

1. The local campaign focuses on local, home-community issues; the national on basic issues of wide, national interest.

2. The national campaign, confronted with the problem of reaching millions of voters as effectively as possible, relies heavily upon television, but also uses every other available medium; the local campaign may ignore television and depend primarily upon house-to-house canvassers and more personal contact.

3. Federal campaigns are restricted in their collection and expenditure of campaign funds; most local campaigns are not.

4. Professional experts are employed to manage and direct national and state campaigns, while many community campaigns are handled by the candidate, the candidate's friends, and volunteers.

Aside from these important differences, many of the techniques and strategies employed in conducting them are very similar, differing only in degree. But taking the differences into consideration, you can see how important it is for you to choose the right means of publicizing your campaign.

The safe rule is this: if you are running for office in a small or medium-sized town or rural community, rely mainly on door-to-door canvassing, direct mail, newspapers, and radio to get your message to the voters. And do a lot of public speaking, handshaking and smiling. Such personal contact work is the key to victory.

Most experts agree, however, that television is the most effective medium to use in a presidential or a senatorial campaign. Through television, the candidate can come into the voter's living room and talk to him intimately. It has given a valuable new dimension to national political campaigning.

A CAMPAIGN OUTLINE

Below is a simplified outline for conducting the work of an average campaign. Each of these steps has been discussed in greater detail in previous chapters.

1. Arrange a meeting of friends and persons who you believe share your ideology and will support your candidacy. Organize a citizens' committee.

2. Prepare a profile of the district, showing partisan registration and ideological commitment to your campaign objectives, as indicated by public opinion polls.

3. Originate a campaign theme and a slogan expressing it. Appoint a campaign manager, secretary, publicity chairman, treasurer or financial chairman, and a chairman to supervise canvassing.

4. Announce your candidacy and campaign program, telling why you think it is needed. Publicize your background and qualifications.

5. Start raising funds and recruiting volunteers. Get organized for action, setting up a speaker's bureau.

6. Open a headquarters as near the center of your district as

possible. Equip it with desks, chairs, filing cabinets, phone, etc.

7. Start getting signatures of registered voters to serve as your sponsors in getting your name on the ballot. Also begin getting written endorsements to use in publicity.

8. Begin holding rallies, coffee hours, and other special events to enlist workers and raise campaign funds.

9. Get your campaign literature ready for the printer. Write a biographical sketch and have photographs made with endorsers for publicity use.

10. Use your volunteer and paid workers to encourage registration of voters through door-to-door canvassing and telephone calls. Have canvassers distribute leaflets or campaign folders at homes, meetings, and supermarkets.

11. Follow up with newspaper publicity, display advertising, direct mail, and radio commercials, pointing up why your constituents should vote for you.

12. Stage pep rallies, demonstrations, and parades to arouse enthusiasm.

13. Conduct a last-minute round of telephone calls to remind supporters to go to the polls and vote.

14. Arrange to have poll watchers at polling places to guard against vote fraud.

15. Publicly thank all who assisted in your campaign. Send thank-you letters to leading supporters.

STARTING WITH AN EXPOSÉ

One of the best ways to launch a local campaign is to initiate a newspaper or radio exposé of a corrupt, dangerous, or otherwise bad situation that needs correction, even before announcing your candidacy. The situation you attack should, of course, be directly related to the office you seek.

This exposé may be made by a committee you have organized, or you may enlist the aid of a member of a newspaper or radio station news staff. Give the person you think can be trusted to make the exposé only enough pertinent facts to incite his or her interest. Offer your information only as a tip, suggesting sources of information for verifying it. Urge further investigation.

In 1973 in Los Angeles, Baxter Ward, a television news broadcaster, initiated an exposé of the way county business was being handled by the Los Angeles County Board of Supervisors, and he won election to the board. Tom Dewey launched an investigation of racketeering in New York and was elected governor. It is a tactic that works in all kinds of campaigns for both low and high offices.

When you find something wrong in your local government, investigate it. Can you think of a way to solve the problem or correct the bad situation? Turn it over in your mind. Discuss it with friends. If it is definitely a live issue, you may be able to capitalize upon it in defeating the official blamed for the situation. *Even if he did not cause it, he may have done little or nothing to solve it. That, too, can be a winning issue.*

Rose Ann Vuich, a Democrat from Dinuba, California, became, in 1976, the first woman ever to be elected to the California State Senate. In her campaign, she used the line described above—that her opponent had done very little to solve a major problem—and defeated him. Her opponent, Ernest Mobley, was a ten-year veteran of the legislature, and he was well known in the district in which they were running. The forty-nine-year-old Vuich, a farmer-accountant and the daughter of Yugoslavian immigrants, had never before been a candidate for elective office, and she had not planned to run in 1976. But the woman who had planned to run withdrew when her husband suffered a heart attack. So Vuich ran as a substitute for her friend.

Investigating Mobley's record, which was generally considered by political writers to be almost unbeatable, Vuich found that he had not authored any important agricultural legislation during his ten years in the legislature, although farming is one of San Joaquin Valley's main industries. So she began hammering away on his neglect of the farmers. This line of attack was potent. She promised to provide leadership in working to solve the problems troubling farmers. She spoke to group meetings, shook numerous hands, and did a lot of personal contact campaigning. She also used television commercials to point up the need for electing a state senator who understood the state's agricultural problems. Her personal canvassing along with her volunteer vote-solicitation proved very effective.

ISSUES AND OFFICES

You will find the information for your local campaigns close at hand. Maureen O'Connor found hers by talking with neighbors and friends and by keeping up with city problems by reading the newspapers. Rose Ann Vuich discovered hers through firsthand experience as a farmer and as a consultant on farm problems in her area, and through checking her adversary's legislative record.

Uncovering basic campaign issues is discussed in chapter 5, but here are particular sources that may aid you in finding relevant local issues:

1. Editorials in your local newspaper
2. Letters to the editor complaining about local problems
3. Protest meetings by taxpayers and other concerned citizens
4. Complaints voiced at city council meetings
5. Complaints before your county bar association
6. Complaints before local labor and trade associations

Campaigning for Mayor or City Council

In a campaign for mayor or city council, your winning issue might be high property taxes, inadequate police or fire protection, municipal graft of some kind, neglect of mass transportation, poor sewage disposal, unpaved streets, shortage of downtown parking facilities, or poor city lighting. It could be some form of discrimination in city employment or residential zoning. Few American cities are perfect. But your problem will be to propose a solution that will not provoke the wrath of the taxpaying public. You must measure each solution you propose by this standard: does the public demand justify the cost?

Of course, official corruption is the most potent vote-getting charge you can make in almost any kind of a campaign. But it is usually the hardest of all to prove without a grand jury or legislative inquiry. Sometimes an investigative news person may bring the corruption to light and open the door for a campaign. But as a candidate you must always be careful to document your facts and not make statements that are too sensational to be believable.

If you are planning to run for city council, you should attend council meetings, get acquainted with the newspaper reporters who cover city hall, and try to get on confidential terms with the secretaries of city officials. It might be advisable for you to employ an investigative newspaper reporter to do some "bird-dog" work for you. As the old-time politicos say, you want to "find where the bones are buried."

Complaints voiced at meetings of the city council or the board of supervisors often provide clues to things that are wrong. Write down in your memorandum book the names of those speaking for complaining groups and talk with them after the meeting. Check the information later with experts who should know. Also check to see if the official you plan to run against is in any way responsible for the situation causing the complaints.

Campaigning for School Board

The formula for a successful school board campaign differs very little from running for any low-level public office. Door-to-door canvassing, direct mail, and newspaper publicity are usually the best media to use in reaching the voters.

The community conflicts that develop into campaign issues most frequently involve high taxes to finance rising school costs; teachers' salaries; busing to achieve racial integration; controversial textbooks or teaching methods; disciplinary practices, paddling, expelling, etc.; and school building programs.

Although forced busing to achieve racial integration is the most heatedly debated issue in many communities, there is often little that a school board candidate can honestly promise to do about it, other than to pledge to go along with a court-dictated order or to appeal to a higher court. In 1977, Bobbi Fiedler, a Los Angeles housewife, won election to the school board by campaigning against a proposed busing plan and promising to appeal to a higher court.

In some communities, the struggle for control of schools is motivated by both ideological and economic reasons. Unionization of teachers is frequently an issue. Another not uncommon issue is the fear of some conservatives that their schools will be used to indoctrinate pupils with liberal or leftist ideology. This has for years been a source of bitter conflict in Los Angeles school board elections, and it is also coming to be an issue of great concern in many other parts of the country. It developed into a bitter clash between parents and the school board in Kanawha County, West Virginia, in 1974–75, where the conflict centered mainly upon certain textbooks used in schools there. During the heated controversy, a school house was bombed and a school bus over-turned. A number of coal miners went on a week-long strike in sympathy with the angry parents protesting board policy.

Use of allegedly obscene school textbooks is another source of conflict. A women's organization, Leadership Action, Inc., has petitioned Congress for legislation banning allegedly obscene books and pictures from schools. Those opposing contend this is censorship.

George Weber, spokesman for the Council for Basic Education of Washington, D.C., was quoted in *Reader's Digest* in 1976 as saying: "The schools increasingly are stepping on people's toes when it comes to religion, politics and sex."

Another growing criticism of public schools in many parts of the United States is that they are not teaching children to read and write. Parents in some communities have organized to urge a return to basics, with greater emphasis on reading, writing, and arithmetic.

To win a school board election campaign in most areas, you must go along with the way a majority of the voters think, or else you must be extraordinarily articulate. Facts are important in these campaigns, but the facts are often clouded by prejudices and emotionalism that are difficult to combat.

Campaigning for a Judgeship

In seeking a judicial office, you will need to establish that you have the educational and legal qualifications and that you also have judicial temperament or a reputation for fairness. Those, of course, are the ideal qualifications. We all know judges who are lacking in one or more of them.

Before running for a judgeship, you should seek endorsements from members of your county bar association and try for an appointment to the bench, unless conditions create an immediate opening. The conditions creating an opening are (1) a vacancy on the bench due to death or retirement of a judge; or (2) a situation arises that casts doubt on a judge's fitness for office.

Judges, being human, do err, and the erring one should be your

target if you are planning to run against an incumbent. Before declaring yourself a candidate against him, check with your local
bar association's committee on judicial fitness (chapter 3 suggests
points to check).

Almost every county bar association has one committee that
maintains a watchful eye over judicial conduct. It usually maintains a dossier on judges who have been targets for complaint.
It may be considering some form of official rebuke for an offending
judge. If, through the committee or otherwise, you can expose
his indiscretions or judicial errors before filing as a candidate, it
will be to your advantage. Anything of this nature occurring after
you have filed will be discounted by some voters as "only politics."

In his interesting and shocking book, *The Bench Is Warped*,
Alvin H. Gershenson has a chapter heading, "Don't run against
this judge or you will wind up in jail." Gershenson proceeds to tell
how a Bell County, Kentucky, judge sent a county prosecutor, who
was a political opponent of his, to jail on an allegedly faked
charge. Eventually, the judge himself was in trouble with the law.
This case was a rarity—you are not likely to wind up in jail for
running against a judge. But you do have to be very careful. Any
legal mistake can be especially embarrassing. For instance, if
campaign contributions and expenditures are not reported on time,
or if your campaign literature fails to bear the name and address
of your campaign committee, as required in some communities,
you could be in trouble.

You should scrutinize all of the campaign activities of your adversary with the same care. Among the most common faults as-
cribed to judges are that they are "too soft" or too lenient in dealing with hard-core, repeat offenders. Law enforcement officers,
both police and prosecuting attorneys, frequently accuse them of
"handcuffing the police" by their strict reliance upon legal techni-
calities that seem to favor the criminal and work against public
protection. They are also accused at times of showing bias or
favoritism, and occasionally some are accused of being too harsh
and unrealistic in sentencing.

Public opinion in many parts of the United States in the late
1970s appears to be swinging toward a tougher policy in dealing
with violent crime. Polls indicate a majority favors capital punish-
ment. Since the will of the majority usually prevails in an election,

you should sample public opinion in your community. Then you will know whether you, as a candidate, are swimming with or against the prevailing current.

In almost any campaign for a judicial office, you will need an impressive list of endorsers, including prominent members of the bar and community leaders. Always try for endorsements by the most respected and trusted members of your community. Beware of using endorsements by lawyers who are widely disliked or mistrusted. A speaker's bureau composed of lawyers and leaders of women's clubs will be especially helpful.

It has been customary in times past for bar associations to sponsor judicial candidates, providing substantial financial help within the limits of election laws. You might be able to get such assistance. But even more helpful would be to have a number of the community's best lawyers on your speaker's bureau staff.

In a city judicial campaign, use radio and television spot commercials, billboards, placards, and newspaper advertising and publicity, and make as many personal appearances before groups as possible. In a small town or rural community, rely heavily on personal contact work.

Campaigning for Law Enforcement Offices

If you campaign for sheriff or prosecuting attorney, you may need to paint a vivid picture of your community's crime problem and propose an improved program for dealing with it. In police work, the big problem that often needs correction is either too many unsolved crimes, failure to respond quickly to emergency calls, or inability to gather proper evidence to convict violators. These all come under the general heading of incompetence. The charge of police brutality is also frequently made. In fact, it is made so frequently and so often without sufficient justification that it lacks credibility with many voters. Consequently that charge is less potent in a political campaign than a charge that an officer has been a failure in investigating or solving certain widely publicized crimes. Publicized crimes usually arouse public emotional concern, and when a sheriff fails to solve one in his area or a prosecutor fails to prosecute, he becomes vulnerable politically.

But developing a strong campaign against either a sheriff or a prosecutor (who usually serves under the title of county or district attorney) requires diligent, careful investigation. Some of the investigatory work may already have been done by a newspaper, a citizens' committee, or a grand jury, but a district attorney or one of his deputies, serving as an advisor to the grand jury, may be able to choke off that type of inquiry.

Politically powerful district attorneys have, however, been found guilty of taking payoffs from criminals and underworld bosses, and have in some cases been sent to prison. Asa Keyes of Los Angeles County was one of those convicted and imprisoned for accepting bribes in the Julian Oil scandals in 1929. He was paroled in 1931 after serving nineteen months in San Quentin.

If you can find evidence indicating that a sheriff or a district attorney has accepted a bribe or any kind of a gift from a person or organization in trouble with the law, you have a real potent campaign issue. Keyes' deputy, Buron Fitts, took an active role in prosecuting Keyes and became his successor as district attorney in Los Angeles County.

In a campaign for either sheriff or district attorney, you should use all of the customary media for getting your image and your program—more effective law enforcement—to the voters. The support of special interest groups can be particularly influential. Both a veterans' committee and a lawyers' committee were very active in Fitts' campaign.

SUCCESSFUL GRASS-ROOTS CAMPAIGNS

Maureen O'Connor's Success

In 1972, Maureen O'Connor was a twenty-five-year-old high school teacher in San Diego, California. She was shocked to discover that many of her students were becoming cynical about elections and other democratic processes. One night she was discussing this with her father when an announcement flashed on television about the upcoming city council election. He suggested that Maureen give her students an example of democracy in action by running for the seat in the second district. She did and won.

How she did it provides a good lesson in campaigning for almost any city or county position. Her sister left college temporarily to manage her campaign. They began by recruiting a large army of volunteer workers, starting with about 400 from Maureen's high school. Eventually, they began to attract older volunteers and finally had approximately 750 working as house-to-house canvassers and office help. Doorbell ringing and telephoning played an important role in her campaign, which was short of money. When the primary ended, she had only $1.19 in her campaign treasury and one opponent, Lou Ridgeway, a fifty-three-year-old businessman, who had strong financial support. During the entire campaign, she spent $8,000 to Ridgeway's $40,000. Yet she won with 52 percent of the vote.

Still serving on the council in 1977, O'Connor credited her election victories to personal contact work and a triple house-to-house canvass by dedicated volunteers.

In her door-to-door calls, she had talked with the residents of the second district about the city's problems and how she proposed to help solve them. Her victory not only demonstrated that this kind of grass-roots campaigning was a winning technique for a city campaign, but it was also a confidence-inspiring lesson in the elective process.

Mrs. Sherman's Second Try

In her first try for the Washington State legislature in 1972, Mrs. Marion Kyle Sherman, an active member of the League of Women Voters and the local Grange, lost by 500 votes. Being a native of the area, having been born in Enumclaw, the largest town in the district (population 4,703), and convinced she could win greater voter support, she decided to try again.

Prior to her second campaign in 1974, she planned carefully. Her husband, an engineer, made a careful statistical analysis of every precinct in the district, showing party registration and voter concerns. The major community interests were found to be inflation, schools, environment, and the growing crime rate. She also learned through this precinct study that many of the citizens were disturbed by a land-use project being planned by a large outside organization. Mrs. Sherman became a spokesman for the group opposing this land-use project.

She spoke before numerous community groups. Although she

was state committeewoman of the Democratic Party, she did not mention this, for a majority of the voters in the district were registered Republican. She took as her slogan, "The Choice for an Honest Change." She used yard signs and house-to-house canvassing to augment her own active campaigning and speaking throughout the district. Her well-planned 1974 campaign was successful.

A Door-to-Door Campaign for Mayor

In 1974, Roseland, New Jersey, had not had a Democratic mayor for nearly seventy years, and when twenty-five-year-old Richard Leonard decided to run for the office, many of the old-timers thought he was wasting his time, for he was a Democrat. He hadn't made any secret of that, and two years earlier had campaigned for city council with the slogan, "Roseland Needs a Two-Party System."

Leonard, however, had found a live issue. He had discovered that many of Roseland's citizens were worried because outside financial interests were planning to open up the town for industrial and commercial development. This would mean construction of a lot of apartment houses. Under the city's regulations, multifamily dwellings were not permitted, and most of the citizens wanted to keep it that way.

Yet while Leonard had found the main citizen concern, he soon learned that his opponent and he were on the same side of the issue. That meant he would have to convince the voters that he was better qualified than his adversary to protect their interests.

He set out to make a house-to-house canvass, beginning his conversations with the line: "What improvements would you suggest for Roseland?"

This question got immediate attention. Leonard then inquired about their jobs and their families and asked for suggestions for improving the local schools, roads, and recreational facilities. He made a note of their suggestions and promised to bring them to the attention of city officials. Later, with the aid of volunteers, he typed replies, reporting what action had been taken. His opponent also made house calls but failed to follow up with letters. Leonard said later he believed the letters made the difference. Out of 2,020 votes cast, he won by 200. Most of his assistance was by volunteers. He estimated he spent $1,500 for printing campaign literature.

Board Member at 17, Chairman at 21

Joseph Canciamilla of Pittsburg, California, believes young persons should begin their political careers at an early age. He should know. He won election to the school board in his city when he was only seventeen. That was in 1972. Less than four years later, he was chairman of the board.

Canciamilla became interested in school board politics when he served as student body representative to the board, attending meetings regularly. Friends urged him to become a candidate for the board. At first he declined, thinking his age would be a bar. But after checking with county and state officials, he decided age was no legal barrier. However, soon after filing, he found himself in competition with a union leader, a physician, a lawyer, a black minister, and a Spanish-American businessman.

Realizing that he would have to conduct an aggressive, personal campaign, he started speaking before various community organizations and going door-to-door getting acquainted and talking about school problems. He spent four hours a day on his house-to-house drive. He used his total campaign fund of $410 for direct mail, printing, radio spots, and newspaper advertising. He distributed leaflets and handout cards to voters. In all of his campaigning, he focused on ways to improve the city's school system without any major increase in taxes.

Canciamilla and the physician both won election to the board. Only the physician, who was an incumbent seeking re-election, got more votes than did the seventeen-year-old. Canciamilla's election demonstrated two things: that young persons can win, and that door-to-door campaigning works in school board elections.

A Special Appeal to Ethnic Groups

Thirty-four-year-old Sandra Hoeh added a new technique to campaigning when, in her first bid for an elective office, she won election to a Milwaukee aldermanic seat in 1975.

Hers was a special effort to woo the ethnic vote. Her analysis of the district had disclosed that it included Jewish, Italian, and other ethnic groups in addition to Milwaukee's German, English, and Scandinavian residents. So she decided to write them special letters. A rabbi volunteered to write the letter she mailed to Jewish voters. Special letters were also sent to faculty members of the Milwaukee branch of the University of Wisconsin, located in the district.

Mrs. Hoeh, who had gained political experience by working in McGovern's presidential campaign, relied heavily on 200 volunteer workers to help her in contacting voters of the district. Before starting her door-to-door canvassing, she got polling lists from party headquarters and used them in selecting and pinpointing the precincts where she most needed votes. She used coffee hours and cocktail parties to raise funds. One cocktail party brought in $750, and an auction helped raise $2,600. As election day grew near, sixty of her volunteers got busy on their home phones, calling voters and reminding them to vote for "Sandy." The nickname was easier to remember than Sandra.

She won 59 percent of the vote, defeating a well-known native of Milwaukee, Gerald Farley, a fifty-four-year-old educational consultant and member of the Milwaukee school board. She credited her victory mainly to speaking before community groups, door-to-door canvassing, telephone solicitation, good newspaper publicity, her special letters, and an efficient, well-organized campaign.

Most of the campaigns cited in this and preceding chapters have been chosen because they show how candidates with little or no experience—especially women and young candidates—have defeated older, more experienced politicians. Often they have done it by a lot of personal campaigning, using volunteers for door-to-door canvassing and telephone solicitation of voters. These tools and techniques helped them win. They can help you win, too.

Index